Mike has been a remark
and his impressive res
has represented the

1981 PGA Tour Player of the Year
1981 Open Champion Golfer of the Year
Texas Golf Hall of Fame Inductee

Mike has successfully transitioned to the business
world while continuing his excellence in the Texas golf
environment for decades. Mike has demonstrated his
longevity as well as a golfing record that has to be
one of Texas' great amateur careers.

—STEVE ELKINGTON

1995 PGA Champion
10-time winner on the PGA Tour
Texas Golf Hall of Fame Inductee

Most of you have been reading Mike's name in the sports
pages for the last 40 years. He has won most every
tournament one can win at the local, state, and national
level, some multiple times. He has won more Texas
Golf Association events than anyone
who has come before him.

—CAROL MANN

38 LPGA wins,
including the 1965 U.S. Women's Open Champion
World Golf Hall of Fame inductee
Texas Golf Hall of Fame inductee

Mike has solidified himself as one of the best
competitive amateurs in Texas golf history.

—MARK BUTTON

Author and golf historian

Mike is one of the best amateur golfers in Texas history. He has an impressive resume, including being a member of the Texas Golf Hall of Fame.

—JOHN GRACE

Member 1975 Walker Cup Team

Texas State Amateur Champion

Texas Golf Hall of Fame Inductee

Probably as accomplished an amateur in the state of Texas that we have had. He is the standard by which we grade ourselves.

—GARY DURBIN

Two-time Texas State Senior Champion

His golf game speaks for itself, but as a fellow competitor, I can't say enough. He's just a gentleman and gets what amateur golf is all about.

—LOUIS STEPHENSON

Texas State Senior Champion

Multiple Texas Senior Player of the Year Winner

THE TOURNAMENT GOLFER'S PLAYBOOK

Change your mind,
Change your life:
The Path of the Tournament Golfer

MIKE BOOKER

2022 © Mike Booker
All rights reserved.

Final edit by AskJanis.com
Cover and text design by Beth Farrell
Text layout by Frankie Lee

Sea Script Company
Seattle, Washington
www.seascriptcompany.com
info@seascriptcompany.com

ISBN: 9798360690153
Library of Congress Control No.: 2022919578

First Printing January 2023

Printed in the United States

PREFACE

Most books written about golf are either by famous golfers or famous mental coaches. I am neither. I am, however, a Tournament Golfer. The concepts in this book are not from a renowned golfer who has made all the right moves. Hardly! Nor has it been written by a famous mental coach. But most famous golfers who write a book typically address the physical aspects of golf, touching only lightly on the mental component.

Likewise, most mental golf coaches have never competed at a high level. They have never stepped over a six-foot putt to win a tournament or qualified for a U.S. Amateur. Don't get me wrong. What they have to say about the mental approach to golf is important, but they probably haven't actually done it. The strategies laid out here are from a competitor who has learned by suffering the outcomes of failing to apply these principles effectively or ignoring them altogether: me. But when I've effectively utilized the concepts discussed in this book, I've had some success. You can, too.

I have competed against and alongside some of the finest Tournament Golfers ever including Jack Nicklaus, Fred Couples, and Arnold Palmer. Through practice and observation, I came to recognize that certain common traits define the Tournament Golfer mindset. I didn't invent them; I just put them all together in one place.

This book is for the golfer who wants better tournament outcomes. If you don't play in golf tournaments and just play for fun, this book will still be helpful. You can pick up some good ideas and improve the way you approach your golf game, and maybe, your life.

I've written principally for the Golfer-Who-Plays-Tournaments who wants to become a Tournament Golfer and for the Tournament Golfer who wants to win more tournaments. *This book is for those who wish to compete.* If competition is not your desire, you may find the "Life Hacks" at the ends of the chapters to be valuable to you off the golf course. Any meaningful accomplishment I have experienced in my business or in my personal life can be traced back to my experiences on the golf course—and what I learned there about myself and others.

I grew up in Downey, California, a suburb of Los Angeles. No one in my family played golf. As a teenager, I couldn't have given you directions to where the nearest golf course might be. Golf was simply not on my radar. But my family supported my love for sports, and I played for my school's basketball, football, and baseball teams.

When I was thirteen, my junior high school had a half-day summer sports program, and I signed up. We played all sports at this camp, which was a perfect match for me, as I played whatever sport was in season. It was a fun camp, and my summer was off to a great start. Then one morning I showed up and Coach Lee Myers, a PE coach who ran the sports camp, said we were going to play golf that day. He had a bunch of old clubs and golf balls laid out. He had drawn three-foot circles out on the football field and placed a broomstick in the center of each circle to mimic a pin location.

I told Coach Myers that I had no interest in golf. None. I told him that I was going to head back home, and I'd see him tomorrow when hopefully this golf thing wouldn't be on the menu. I turned and took a couple of steps toward home. Behind me I heard Coach say, "That's okay, Book, go on home! You wouldn't be any good at golf anyway!" As I turned to make some sort of smart-ass comment, with a big grin on his face, he stuck a club in my hand. A week later I had my own set of (used) clubs. I told my baseball, basketball, and football coaches thank-you very much, but I was done with their sport and wouldn't be playing them anymore. And I never did again!

Coach Lee Myers

Coach Myers and I began a close father–son-like relationship that day, which lasted many years. Since my dad left our home when I was two, he was just the man I needed at just the right time in my life. He traveled to tournaments with me, often as my caddie. When I hit tenth grade and would be going to high school, Coach Myers applied for the golf coach job at my high school and got it. Now, we would go to high school together. I spent hours and hours at his apartment with him and Mrs. Myers, often eating dinner together while discussing golf. Lee Myers was a scratch player—and we played together most every week. Our rounds together were some of the most important golf lessons and life lessons I would ever receive.

When I was sixteen, I made it to the semifinals of the California match play. I had been playing a little over three years and had virtually no tournament experience. I was just a kid who was playing really well with no particular awareness or game plan for what I was doing. I was simply playing golf. My opponent in the semis was none other than Scott Simpson, the famous junior golfer who would go on to win two NCAA individual titles and sixteen professional wins, including a U.S. Open.

Scott duck-hooked his drive out of bounds on the 1st and 2nd holes for a double-bogey/double-bogey start. I won both holes easily. I remember standing on the 3rd tee box thinking, *I wonder who I'll play in the finals?* This is my first memory of being a Golfer-Who-Plays-Tournaments. Instead of staying in the present and focusing on the task at hand, my mind had raced far into the future.

Scott, already an accomplished Tournament Golfer, was calm and cool on the third tee box. I remember that, too! While I was wondering who I might be playing in the finals, he was planning how to correct his duck hook and get his swing back on track. Scott was completely in the present.

You can figure out how this ended. Scott closed our match out on the 16th hole, beating me 3 and 2. He went on to win in the finals. I was a Golfer-Who-Plays-Tournaments who went up against a Tournament Golfer, wondering what just happened.

In that same year, I represented my high school in the state high school championship known as CIF (California Interscholastic Federation). Coach Myers, my new high school coach/one-man gallery, and I drove down to San Diego to play. In the first round of the tournament, I hit three consecutive balls out of bounds on the 2nd hole and carded a six-over-par 10 on a par-four hole.

When I found my first ball, it was just six inches out of bounds. My second ball was about a yard out of bounds. I never found the third ball, but I was devastated. I didn't finish dead last, but it was a tough experience, nonetheless. For days, I focused on the fact that my first ball was so close to being in-bounds. What if it had ended up just six inches to the left and in-bounds? Everything would have been different. What I wasn't ready to admit was that it was I who had made the 10—no one else. Rather than take responsibility for my actions, I blamed the unfairness of it all— the unfairness of golf.

I was not ready to be a Tournament Golfer like Scott was. I was unable to stay in the present in my match with him, and

I was likewise unable to accept that I was the one who kept hitting it out of bounds in the state high school championship. What I didn't understand then was that golf had much more to teach me. Tournament Golfers compete in the present and take responsibility for all that happens. I had no idea any of this existed.

Golf can be solitary and even lonely. Competing in tournament golf is dramatically more isolating. Ultimately, it's just you and the ball. Unlike team sports, no one can set a pick for you so that you can drive to the basket for an easy layup. No one is there to make a great catch from your poorly thrown football. It's just you. You suffer directly from your errors, and you benefit directly from your accomplishments. But there's no sugar-coating it. Golf is difficult.

If I'm being perfectly honest, I only became a true Tournament Golfer in the last thirty years or so. When I say *true* Tournament Golfer, I mean that I had always displayed some Tournament Golfer characteristics—but not reliably or with purpose. It was a challenge for me to put four tournament rounds together often enough to be a consistent winner. I would finish a tournament feeling that I hit the ball well and made my share of putts but didn't get it done for some reason. I usually couldn't figure out why.

More importantly, when I did win an event, I couldn't always explain why I won. It's a fact that we learn from our mistakes. But winning teaches us important things, too, and I wasn't paying attention to why I won. I believed I was a Tournament Golfer, but I was still a Golfer-Who-Plays-Tournaments.

There is nothing in the pages that follow that is going to change anything about the difficulty—the cruelty—that golf has in store for all of us. We all signed on for it. My aim is to lay out a path to play golf, especially tournament golf, with an entirely different mindset than you may be currently using. Are you a Tournament Golfer or a Golfer-Who-Plays-Tournaments? If you're not sure, then you may be a Golfer-Who-Plays-Tournaments.

That's totally fine. In this book, I will spend most of my time defining the attributes of Tournament Golfers and how they differ from Golfers-Who-Play-Tournaments. I have observed these two types of players over many years of competitive golf. Both golfers play golf tournaments, and both may have great skill. But if you play tournament golf, I believe your success will depend on your ability to become and maintain the core elements of the Tournament Golfer. You've got this! Read on!

CONTENTS

Printed book and eBook available at:

For more information about
The Tournament Golfer's Playbook, visit:

tgplaybook.com

info@tgplaybook.com

2012 Senior Champion
MIKE BOOKER

ACKNOWLEDGEMENTS

Having an idea for a book is one thing. Turning that idea into a book is quite another. The experience is as challenging as it is rewarding. I especially want to thank the individuals that helped make *The Tournament Golfer's Playbook* happen through their interactions with me on and off the course.

I have to start by thanking my remarkable wife, Patty. From reading early drafts to giving me advice on the book's tone, its message and even the look of the front cover, she was with me the whole way, as always.

Complete thanks to Coach Leland Myers who changed the trajectory of my life on the athletic field one summer day. It's no exaggeration to say that if he hadn't introduced me to the game of golf, there's no telling where I'd be today—or if I'd be here today. Thank you, Coach!

Love and kisses to my mother, Dorothy Booker, for the hundreds of chauffeured trips back and forth to the golf course before I reached legal driving age. And thanks, Mom, for giving me this enduring advice: "As long as you try your best, you will always be able to look yourself in the mirror." Love you, Mom. Miss you.

Love and deep gratitude to Carol Mann, World Golf Hall of Fame member, who's unwavering belief in me was steadfast and true. "Failure is not the opposite of success, Mike; it is merely a steppingstone to success."

Many thanks are also in order to Coach Dave Williams, venerable University of Houston golf coach. Coach Williams created the greatest Division One golf program the world has ever known, and I was fortunate to be a small part of it. I'll always be a Cougar.

Thank you to Steve and Tom, my first golf buddies and lifelong friends. Also, my golf support group at River Oaks CC: Charlie, Titus, Jared, Brad, Larry, David, Gregg, Drew, and Jimmy. And my Texas posse that I have competed against and with for over forty years: Pat Youngs, Bob Kearney, John Pierce, Mike Rice, Gary Durbin, John Grace, Jack Tyson, Mark Pease, and Scott Smith to name just a few. These guys can really play the game and I am grateful to call them friends.

Thanks to Kathy Walton, philanthropist and business pioneer, who has been an inspiration and shining light in my life. Things are always better when you are around.

Thank you to the amazingly talented team at Financial Synergies whose unmatched abilities to care for our clients in my absence has afforded me the flexibility to pursue tournament golf in my spare time.

Finally, I thank God for the people mentioned above and whose guiding hand sustains me through this life.

My grace is sufficient for you,
for my power is made perfect in weakness.
—2 Corinthians 12:9

To Pat and Caitlin,
whose laughter is like sugar—it makes my life sweeter.

To Coach Leland Myers,
whose belief in me allowed me to believe in myself.

And to my mother, Dorothy.
Mom, I would have made a terrible doctor. . .
people would have died.

1

RECREATIONAL GOLF vs. TOURNAMENT GOLF

If you watch a game, it's fun. If you play it,
it's recreation. If you work at it, it's golf.

—Bob Hope

There's a considerable difference between recreational golf and tournament golf.

RECREATIONAL GOLF

You drink a few beers, have some laughs and a fun day with your foursome. Only the players in your group will know how well or how badly you scored. In fact, you may not even keep score. No significant stress before or after the round. Recreational golf is what most golfers play, and it's great. There's no better way to have fun with your friends or to get to know people than playing recreational golf. I love recreational golf, and I love playing it!

TOURNAMENT GOLF

This version of golf is more serious. You always keep score and must attest to that score when the round is completed. If you get that score wrong, you might even be disqualified and essentially get yourself kicked out of the tournament. Because there is greater potential for a substantially larger pool of people to know how well or how badly they played, there is correspondingly greater pressure in tournament golf than in recreational golf. Though the starter on the 1st tee at a tournament may say, "Have fun out there," the Tournament Golfer isn't playing for fun. The Tournament Golfer plays for the challenge, the trophy. Because so many more people know how the Tournament Golfer fared in an event, it dramatically magnifies either the negative for a poor outing or the positive for a good outing. Results are routinely put online for the whole world to see. That's pressure. I love tournament golf, and I love playing it, too. It is, however, a unique form of golf and differs greatly from recreational golf.

Entering a golf tournament comes with certain expectations. Some players want to make the cut; some just want to play the famous golf course hosting the event. Some players want to be tested, while others want to win. Tournament Golfers know what they want before they hit the first shot of a competition. They might be *hoping* for a good outcome and that's okay, but they also know what they want from the tournament experience. *Knowing* is richer and deeper than wishful thinking or hoping.

Tournament golf brings out the best and the worst in us. Too many experiences of seeing ourselves at our worst can inspire positive change or turn us away from tournament golf altogether. Golf has much to teach the willing; but tournament golf is a master's-level class of learning who we are and what we are capable of—the good and the not so good.

Recreational golf, especially for those who are relatively new to the game, is primarily a physical endeavor. Beginners are just trying to make decent contact with the ball. Most recreational golfers spend the majority of their time and energy in perfecting their swing and may not focus on the mental component very much. As they improve and begin to get more consistent, their attention will migrate to the mental side of golf, including course management. After all, once a ball can be hit on a green from various yardages with some sort of consistency, recreational golfers are left to wonder why they can't do it all the time. Golfers at all levels are trying to figure this out, too.

2

THE
GOLFER-WHO-PLAYS-TOURNAMENTS
AND THE TOURNAMENT GOLFER

He that is good at making excuses is
seldom good for anything else.

—Benjamin Franklin

The Golfer-Who-Plays-Tournaments always has a list of excuses for any poor score, and it can be quite extensive. I'm certain you've heard some of these before:

"I had six lip-outs today!"

"My back was killing me."

"I got the worst bounces today."

"I never catch a break."

"I had a terrible pairing."

Look, I'm not saying their back wasn't killing them or that they didn't have six lip-outs. What I'm saying is that the Tournament Golfer has no list of excuses. The Tournament Golfer just gives the score when asked. No drama, just a number. Coach Dave Williams, legendary golf coach at the University of Houston, would famously ask his players how we stood to par during our round of a tournament. If we started to explain all the bad breaks we had or lipped-out putts, he was quick to tell us, "No weather reports, boys, just your score!" He was molding us into Tournament Golfers, and we didn't even realize it.

Tournament Golfers are not necessarily tough by nature, but they are particularly tough in tournaments. When I say tough, I really mean *disciplined*. Discipline comes in many forms, and it may not be the way you would traditionally define the word. We have talked about the discipline of avoiding excuses—"Don't complain, don't explain." But Tournament Golfers also have the discipline of preparing for an upcoming tournament by being honest with themselves as to what component of their game needs the most attention. Too often, Golfers-Who-Play-Tournaments go out and bang balls, neglecting other areas of their game that may need work, such as putting and short game.

Tournament Golfers know that to dwell on the negative only hurts themselves. If they triple the 18th hole to shoot par, they just say, "72" when asked what they shot. The Golfer-Who-Plays-Tournaments might say, "I tripled 18 for a 72," and wait for the acknowledgement of their victimhood. Tournament Golfers haven't got time for that. They are on their way to the driving range to work some things out.

Golfers-Who-Play-Tournaments are convinced the universe is lined up against them. They take no responsibility for anything that happens on the golf course—and maybe off the course, too. They are victims of bad breaks, bad luck. Webster's Dictionary defines luck as "success or failure apparently brought by chance rather than through one's own actions." I don't want my golf dependent on luck at all. Fact is, I don't believe in the concept of luck. It just isn't healthy to blame bad results on some outside agency or to praise that outside agency for shots that came off as planned. What a crazy way to think.

THE '99 U.S. AMATEUR

In 1999, I played in the U.S. Amateur at Pebble Beach. In the thirty-six-hole, on-site qualifier, I was paired with one Tournament

Golfer and one Golfer-Who-Plays-Tournaments. Their view of things couldn't have been more diverse. I was impressed with the Tournament Golfer when he struck beautiful drive after beautiful drive, but on the 10th hole he got an outrageously bad kick off the edge of a sprinkler, careening dead right into six-inch rough. You know it was a remarkably straight drive because the sprinkler head he hit the side of, like most fairway sprinkler heads, was located right down the center of the fairway. I looked over at him and his expression provided no evidence that he was upset or that he even cared about this terrible bounce his ball just experienced. To add insult to injury, he had one of the worst lies I had seen the whole week. He had no drama, no whining. He just chopped the ball back out in the fairway and went about his business. I don't remember if he made par on that hole, but he qualified and made it to match play.

My other playing partner, the Golfer-Who-Plays-Tournaments, couldn't have been more different. He whined all day—about the weather, about his hotel room, about his caddie, his [fill in the blank]. Our group finally reached the famous 18th hole at Pebble. *Everyone* knows you don't mess with the left side; it's the Pacific Ocean out there. The Tournament Golfer and I hit it down the right side, just left of the famous cypress tree. Our Golfer-Who-Plays-Tournaments started it too far left out over this cliff's edge trying to hit a cut. Unless the breeze off the cove was going to push it right, this ball was taking a swim. The breeze did not assist, and the ball went in the ocean.

He went nuts! "What a terrible break! I've been getting screwed all day!" and on and on. The Tournament Golfer and I looked at each other, both of us thanking God that this was the last hole we would have to play with this loser. Nothing good ever happens to the Golfer-Who-Plays-Tournaments, I guess.

SHOULD I GO PUT MY SPIKES ON?

Now, your club or the course you play is chock-full of Golfers-Who-Play-Tournaments. They are the ones who take you through every shot they hit in their last round. When they finish, you might think they would have shot the course record if not for their bad luck. When these golfers would begin to tell my University of Houston teammate and friend, Ed Fiori, all their golf shots beginning at the 1st tee, he would ask them if he should go put his golf shoes on—because he figured their story could take a while. Like me, he couldn't bear to hear the entire play-by-play of someone's round. Just give us the number and get on with it. One good story or shot, fine; but not every shot.

PAIRED WITH THE TOURNAMENT GOLFER

Of all the great players I have competed against, Lindy Miller was the calmest guy I have ever been paired with. He was, and still is, a Tournament Golfer. His teammates called him "Log" for his legendary ability to sleep anywhere, anytime. Of all the legendary players that Oklahoma State produced, Lindy is one of the very best. He played the PGA Tour for several years, and as an amateur he won several major amateur events. He was Low Amateur in the 1977 U.S. Open and Low Am the next year at The Masters. He is a member of the Texas Golf Hall of Fame.

I mention Lindy because he is one of the best examples of a Tournament Golfer. He never got too excited about the bad things or the good things that happened to him during a tournament round. In 1977, he was at the top of his game, and we were paired together in the All-America Intercollegiate hosted by my team at the University of Houston. He played fairly well the first thirteen holes but was getting nothing out of his round. He was even par but, by all rights, should have been under par. You couldn't tell that he was frustrated from his demeanor—no club-throwing, no whining. He was patient.

Sure enough, he birdied the last five holes in a row for a sweet 67. After the round, his teammates gathered around him. He just told them his score and went to get something to eat. No explanations, no drama. Just another day at the golf course. Had I done what he did, I would have had five different stories about what I had just pulled off. But Lindy was *clinical*. He was part of my journey to begin to understand that there were indeed two types of people who played tournaments: the Tournament Golfer and the Golfers-Who-Play-Tournaments. Lindy was a Tournament Golfer.

THE GUN FIGHTER

In some ways, a Tournament Golfer is analogous to the gun fighter depicted in a Western movie. Like the Gun Fighter who is constantly challenged by the new kid in town who's looking for a showdown to update their Gun Fighter resume, the Tournament Golfer enters competitions where their skill and resolve are also tested again and again. With every tournament entered, the Tournament Golfer faces a new test—a new collection of trials. The Gun Fighter doesn't necessarily enjoy gunning down their opponent, but like the Tournament Golfer, they have an inner calling to repeatedly prove themselves. Both get wounded along the way, too—that's part of the contract they signed when they first started. The trick is to survive each encounter.

My point is, neither the Gun Fighter nor the Tournament Golfer do what they do for fun. They do it for the challenge. And when things go badly, everyone in town finds out. This also comes with the territory. There is a dichotomy at play for both individuals, too. When a tournament is over, there is the sense of relief and, at the same time, a yearning for the next event to get under way. Of course, the Gun Fighter is grateful to have prevailed in the fight, but soon begins to wonder when and where the next shootout will be.

The Gun Fighter and the Tournament Golfer are likewise solitary participants. Sometimes in a Western, the Gun Fighter may get a little help when outnumbered, but the Tournament Golfer is always alone in the fight.

Life Hack

Life is tough. It's easy to fall into the habit of making excuses because it really isn't natural to blame ourselves for things that happen to us, to forget we may have some responsibility in those experiences. Often, "bad breaks," as we call them, seem to just fall out of the sky and are beyond our control. In life, there are bad things that happen, which are, indeed, not caused directly by our actions. Recently, I was stopped at a red light and the car behind me rear-ended me. Clearly, this was not something I brought upon myself. The greatest of Tournament Golfers doesn't overly care if they caused their bad break or not. Their focus is on acceptance and how they are going to deal with the new situation in real time.

I'm a Tournament Golfer. I don't feel sorry for myself. It doesn't help me to waste time dwelling on something that already happened, something in the past. Truth is, it would make things dramatically worse if I wasted time on being angry or upset. Because as soon as it happened, it was in the past—ancient history. I accepted the situation for what it was and set about fixing the problem.

At work, I make presentations to clients and prospective clients. In live interactions with people, it's easy to say the wrong thing or to totally forget to say the right thing. When I make these presentations, and they choose not to sign on the line, I don't make excuses. I get feedback where possible and go on to the next meeting, the next prospect. Taking what I learned from the last meeting, I apply it to the next meeting. It's like making a strategy decision in a tournament to avoid sucker pins (those pins that only the bold or the foolish aim for). You learn and adapt. Like golf, learn from mistakes and keep going forward without excuses or wasting time wondering "what if." This is the essence of the Tournament Golfer mindset *off the course*.

When you find yourself in a difficult situation off the course, don't make excuses, don't whine. Nobody wants to hear your excuses anyway. You're a Tournament Golfer.

3
FORGET ABOUT RESULTS
FOCUS ON PROCESS

I can go to that putting green now and make twenty straight three-footers. And then, you get to the course, and you feel a little different and you can't do what you normally do.

—Ernie Els

There is a debate in golf as to what a player should be thinking when preparing for a shot. There are two schools of thought.

RESULTS-ORIENTED

This philosophy suggests picturing the result and plugging it into your brain to achieve the result. It is situational. See the putt go in prior to the stroke and focus on that result. See the drive hit the middle of the fairway before taking the club back, plugging that image into your brain. Every swing is unique and situational. Focus on the result and a process of some sort will appear and the desired result will happen. This approach requires thinking in terms of an outcome: the future.

PROCESS-ORIENTED

This philosophy advocates picking your target, visualizing the shot, stepping up and pulling the trigger. The emphasis is the process of hitting the shot. It is self-contained. Every swing has the same value—with no swing being any more important than another. There is no thought of consequences or result. Your focus is on the process, letting the result come about from that process.

This approach requires thinking in terms of process—staying in the present.

Process is the foundation of the Tournament Golfer. Winners and losers have the same goal. Winners simply have a better process. Process is identical every time you step up to the ball. Process is your home, your safe place, especially under pressure. Ever wonder why you can step up on the practice range and hit the ball beautifully only to find that on the course you can't hit it at all? Or when on the practice putting green, you will nonchalantly tap in a three-foot putt every time, but on the course, it's another matter?

The answer is that on the range, you're all process. There is no scorecard. Once on the course, it is an entirely different matter. There is a scorecard, and you want *results*! When golfers play results-oriented golf, they often worry about the consequences of a poor swing, a poor shot, or even a poor round. They get tense and no longer act; they are forced to react. Under tournament pressure, focusing on a particular result or consequence instead of on the process is the fundamental nature of failing under pressure: choking.

When Tournament Golfers are on the 18th tee box with a one-stroke lead on the last round of the tournament, they are focused on making the same swing they have been making since the first swing of the event. The Golfer-Who-Plays-Tournaments, on the other hand, is trying to find a way to make a par so they can win the tournament. They are reacting to a situation and are focused on a result, on an outcome. Whenever you see a tour player ready to hit a shot and then they suddenly step away from the ball, they have caught themselves thinking about result; they are wisely resetting themselves.

JACKIE BURKE WISDOM

"Never try to make a putt, Booker. Ever."

This is what Jackie Burke, Masters champion and World Golf Hall of Fame inductee, told me forty-three years ago; and when he said it, I thought he had lost his mind. I had called him earlier that morning to ask if I could come over for a putting lesson. I was having real putting problems, and Mr. Burke had always been encouraging to me in the few encounters we had. He told me to come on over.

When I arrived at Champions Golf Club for my lesson, the sky turned black, and it began to pour. He motioned me into his office and my putting lesson began on his oriental rug in front of his desk. The lesson began with him critiquing my stroke, which he liked. I hit many putts and made a few changes per his direction. Then we moved into his mental approach. It was then he dropped the bomb: *Never try to make a putt*!

This advice was pure wisdom. Without coming out and saying it, Mr. Burke was introducing me to *process*, not *result*. As he went on to explain, he took one of the golf balls and drew a two-inch straight line on it. He told me my only job was to roll the stripe he had drawn on the ball down my selected line. "Once you hit the ball, your job is done [process]. That's all you can do. Worrying about making the putt [result] just complicates your stroke and you won't make anything."

This advice was the greatest golf advice—the best insight—I have ever received.

While my respect for Mr. Burke's advice was high, I was too inexperienced to understand the immense weight of what he had just told me. I'm grateful that years later his sage advice finally resonated with me, and I have been able to benefit from it. I *never* try to make a putt. If you're a Tournament Player, you shouldn't try either.

In summary, results-oriented players visualize the line of their putts, visualize the ball going in the hole, and then try to make the putt. Process-oriented players also visualize the line of their putt, but roll the ball down their selected line with no thought of the outcome. This golfer is just rolling the ball down the line, not trying to "make the putt." If the putt drops, great, but process-oriented players are not preoccupied with the result of the putt dropping or not. They know that after the putt is struck, they have no control over the outcome. They surrender to the outcome.

Ask yourself this: Who has the better chance of making a putt on the last hole to win a tournament? The golfer who is consumed with the result of what making this putt will mean to them if it drops? Or the golfer who is simply rolling their stripe down the selected line?

KENNY PERRY

Kenny Perry was perhaps the best player on the PGA Tour to have never won a Major Championship. He racked up 14 tour wins, pocketed over $32 million in career earnings, won ten Champions Tour events and was a Ryder Cup team member. In 2009, he seemed destined to add a Major to his distinguished resume, The Masters. Perry was the 54-hole leader and held that lead with two holes to go. "On 16, I hit it to six inches for birdie," Perry says. "I tapped it in, and I looked over at the scoreboard and I immediately said to myself, 'Hummm, I'm two up with two to play.' My whole thought process all week was this saying of being 'aggressively patient.' And all of the sudden I said to myself, 'If you make two pars, you win the Masters.' It hit me. All of a sudden, I went from being aggressive to tentative."

When the scoreboard beckoned him to the future, Perry abandoned his process and switched his mind to result-oriented thinking. He promptly made bogeys at 17 and 18 to relinquish his lead.

"It's funny how your mind changes," he would later admit. "I went from being in the moment—I had it, I was sharp—to all of a sudden saying, 'All I have to do is make two pars.' It just changed my whole world—the way I was thinking, the way I was feeling. Shoot, I was 2 up with two to play. I gave it away, I just choked."

This set up a sudden-death playoff for the title with Angel Cabrera and Chad Campbell. Campbell was eliminated on the first extra hole with a bogey. Cabrera became Masters champion with a par on the second extra hole as Kenny missed the green for another bogey.

Even legendary players the likes of Kenny Perry can fail to realize that their process has been compromised by thoughts of a result. The Tournament Golfer expects result-oriented thinking to come front-and-center when under pressure and has trained themselves to deal with it. I will examine some effective techniques in later chapters to help you maintain your process orientation when the "result monster" comes to crash the party.

WILT THE STILT, ET AL.

Results-oriented techniques have failed in other sports, too. One example is Wilt Chamberlain, the famous L.A. Laker center. He was an incredible offensive force in his career in the NBA. He is still the only center in history to lead the league in assists, averaging over 50 points for a season and scoring 100 points in a single game. However, 11,862 times in his NBA career, he was at the free-throw line and 5,805 times, he was unable to put more points on the scoreboard. The season he averaged over 50 points, he got to the free-throw line over fifteen times per game yet made only ten of his attempts. He admitted he was a headcase at the free-throw line.

I would say Mr. Chamberlain was—at the free-throw line at least—a results-oriented player. Instead of focusing on the process of shooting the ball as he would during regular play, he became a headcase because he was so afraid of a bad result—missing the free throw. He was intentionally fouled more than any other player because his free-throw percent was barely north of fifty percent. Therefore, these intentional fouls were always at key moments of a game when a Chamberlain miss at the line could result in a loss for the Lakers. He could not help but think that a missed free throw would result in a loss for his team. Ironically, his results would have been substantially better if he had perfected his process, focused on process and not worried about the result of a miss.

Bill Buckner was a gifted baseball player who had over 2,700 hits in his stellar career in big league baseball. But in the 9th inning of game six of the 1986 World Series, Buckner went to field a routine ground ball hit by Mookie Wilson. As Buckner approached the ball, it rolled between his legs and into right field. Ray Knight scored from second base, giving the New York Mets the win to even the series at 3–3. Billy Buckner forgot about his process in fielding a routine ground ball by thinking of the result of the game ending with his throw to 1st base. When he approached the ball to field it, he jumped from process to result. The outcome was disastrous—the ball rolled through his legs and into the outfield.

After beating the Dallas Cowboys defense, DeSean Jackson ran towards the end zone following a sixty-yard pass from Donovan McNabb. Inexplicably, just before reaching the goal line, Jackson threw the ball behind him in celebration. No touchdown. The Eagles managed to score with a one-yard touchdown run by Brian Westbrook on the next play but would go on to lose the game to Dallas. DeSean threw his process of crossing into the end zone out the window and began celebrating his result, which turned out to be anything but the result he wanted.

The same is true for those golfers suffering from putting yips, the dreaded jerky stroke that causes an otherwise "gimmie" putt to be missed. If you have ever seen a player with the yips or if you suffer from the yips yourself, you know that this malady shows up exclusively on short putts. All too often, a player with even the most severe case of the yips will make beautiful strokes on longer, lag putts. Most of us are happy to get a forty-foot putt within three feet. Why such a different mindset with longer putts versus short putts? Obviously, we are much more inclined to be results-oriented with the shorter putt we expect to make—which we *should* make. We are trying to make the short putt and just stroking the ball toward the hole on long putts. By expecting to make the short putt, the anticipation puts us in results-oriented mode, which is exclusively outcome-focused. People with putting yips are not living in the present.

Life Hack

I remember trying to lose ten pounds a few years back. I would weigh myself every morning to see if my new diet was working. I was so focused on my goals that I wasn't paying much attention to my day-to-day process of eating a lesser volume of high-calorie foods. I was snaking here and there, thinking it didn't have much negative impact on my weight-loss program. The problem was, I really needed to adjust my process, and eliminate all the excess snacking, if the pounds were going to start falling off. I started weighing myself less often, and tightened up my process—with just one snack during the day and no snacks after 6:00 P.M. Adjusting my process with less daily attention to the scale enabled me to lose the weight. My process delivered my desired result.

We all have work goals and life goals. At my firm, I advocate to all new advisors that if they will focus on taking care of the client, everything will come to them: the money they wish to make, the impact they will have on their family, and the overall fulfillment they seek in their work.

Success lies in the process. The result you want to happen will happen naturally as a byproduct of your attention to the process.

4
BEING IN THE PRESENT

Do not dwell in the past; do not dream of the future;
concentrate the mind on the present moment.

—The Buddha

STAYING IN THE PRESENT MOMENT

Everything I have talked about has led to this point: being in the present. This is the essence of the Tournament Golfer. The Tournament Golfer is a process-oriented individual who operates in the present. Zen Buddhism refers to this state as mindfulness. Only the present is recognized—the body and mind are in sync. Tournament Golfers might call it "being in the zone."

As author Myrko Thum says, the present moment is all there truly is:

The present moment is the only thing where there is no time. It is the point between past and future. It is always there, and it is the only point we can access in time. Everything that happens, happens in the present moment. Everything that ever happened and will ever happen can only happen in the present moment. It is impossible for anything to exist outside of it.

Being present is complicated because we are always encouraged to think about the future or to dwell on our past. Our culture encourages us to live in the past where we often edit out the unpleasant parts, making our past remembered as better than it was. Or, we are encouraged to live for the future as we set our reminders and notifications on our phones for events that have not yet taken place.

There is great value in remembering and reliving our past successes and mistakes, to learn from them. Likewise, we couldn't effectively make our way through the world if we never planned or prepared for possible future outcomes. The Tournament Golfer spends time learning from the past, makes adjustments, and visualizes what the future might bring. The Golfer-Who-Plays-Tournaments focuses too intently on the past, beating themselves up over the mistakes made and worries about the future.

Think about the past in small doses, and make sure the reason you're there is a positive one. Do the same for the future—small doses, for low-anxiety reasons. Aiming to spend time in the present while balancing time between the past and future is the key to successful tournament golf and a healthy life.

While on the course, how many times have you carried a double bogey around with you to the back nine, which happened on the front nine? In doing so, you're stuck in the past. How many times have you worried about a hole coming up and forgotten to play the hole you are on? In doing so, you are getting ahead of yourself, stuck in the future.

GOING THROUGH THE MOTIONS

How often have you eaten a meal and not really tasted it or driven to work without really thinking about it? Our days often pass us by while our minds are elsewhere. Being in the moment is really challenging. Often, the harder you try to be in the moment, the farther away from the present you get. How do you get in the present? How do you stay in the present?

Watch a young child. There is no better example. A two-year-old doesn't think about what happened to them yesterday or what the plan is later in the day. If a two-year-old gets angry, they can go over the top and, in that moment, nothing else in the world matters but what angered them. After the crying is over, they soon return to normal with the reason for getting upset long forgotten. Don't throw a tantrum, but having a child's mind on the course is a great way to be: No worries about the last shot, and no thoughts about a shot not yet taken.

TOUR SCHOOL

In 1981, I was at the final stage of the PGA tour school again at Waterwood National, a beast of a course designed by Pete Dye. Back then, the top twenty-five finishers earned their tour membership. I was playing well and made the cut. Going into the back nine, I felt I was somewhere near the top twenty-five bubble. It had been a steady rain all day. Conditions were difficult. But I was thinking I needed another birdie coming in. On the 15th hole, I hit my approach shot into a monkey grass bush and made double bogey. Now I thought I needed to birdie at least two of the remaining three holes to have a chance at my tour card.

I focused all my energy on birdies. If I made a bogey now, it really didn't matter; to my mind, I was now outside the bubble, so who cared if bogeys took me farther outside the bubble? The pin was cut front edge on 16, and I came up a yard short trying to get it close. My ball spun back and into the bunker. In trying to hole the bunker shot out for the needed birdie, I hit it a foot from the hole for an easy par. But par isn't what I needed. On 17, I ran at a fifteen-foot putt by the hole four feet and started to putt out. It no longer mattered if I made a bogey as I tried to make a birdie. I marked my ball and waited my turn. I casually knocked my second putt in for par. On 18, I ran at a birdie yet again, running it well past the hole a few feet. Again, I started to hurriedly finish the putt out. The rain was picking up, and it was getting cold. Having failed to get my tour card, I just wanted to go home and lick my wounds. I went ahead and marked my ball and waited my turn. Once again, I made the par putt as if I were messing around with my friends in a dollar putt-putt game.

I signed my scorecard, and my wife Pat and I went to get something to eat before the drive home. I had no hint of a life after golf, so we discussed what I might do for a living. What exactly was my Plan B? As she tells it, the "cut arrow" on the scoreboard that was behind me was steadily dropping to include ever-higher scores to be included in the top twenty-five. She didn't let on that this was going on right behind me. After our food arrived, she told me to be quiet and motioned over my shoulder. The cut arrow had dropped far enough to include my name. I was in the top twenty-five finishers, and I'd earned my tour card on the number.

I have often wondered what scores I would have recorded on the last three holes had someone come over to me on the 16 tee box and said, "Hey, Booker, just par the last three holes to get your tour card." This would have pulled me out of being present, changing my focus from process to results. Because of the double bogey on 15, I had surrendered to the probable outcome of not qualifying, so it was natural to stay in the present with every swing coming in.

There were a couple of important lessons I learned from this experience. It is a battle to get into and stay in the present. The only way to do that is to work the process, avoiding thoughts of consequences. When I was aggressively running those putts well past the hole, I couldn't have cared less about the consequences of 3-putting because I was in the moment of making the best stroke I could make. The second lesson is as old as time: Never give up—because you never know what good things can happen if you just keep punching.

Life Hack

Remember the past but don't live there. Plan for the future but don't ignore the present. Begin the process and habit of recognizing when you repeatedly pull the past into your present. Past experiences, good or bad, can overwhelm your present. Endeavor to spend most of your time in the present. Plan for the future but try not to obsess about it. "What worries you," John Locke wrote, "masters you." This statement continues to be true. Each of us has worried about a bad thing happening at a future date, only to find out that it was all a waste of time, effort, and stress.

My daughter Caitlin traveled 1,575 miles away from us for her freshman year of college at The College of the Holy Cross in Worcester, Massachusetts. Cait had always been an accomplished student in high school with an enviable GPA. A few weeks into her first semester, Pat and I received a panicked phone call on a Monday night. Her professor had asked her to come a few minutes early to the next class being held the following Wednesday. He wanted to discuss the paper she had turned in. It sounded ominous.

She checked and rechecked her paper and determined that one or two of her footnotes were not perfect. He was a real stickler for accurate footnotes and told the class any paper that didn't properly credit its sources would be considered plagiarism. Like most parents, we assured her that all would be okay. She had done her best and, after all, she was a skilled writer with a solid history of exceptional writing. When we hung up the phone, however, we began to wonder ourselves. Isn't it just a little odd that he asked her to come in early? Why not just give her a lower grade for inadequate footnotes? Pretty soon, we began to worry, too. Could she get expelled for plagiarism? If so, what school would take her? And how would she explain that it was just a sloppy footnote and not really plagiarism?

All three of us had a sleepless night that night. All day Tuesday, I worried for Cait. I couldn't focus on my work at the office. Pat told me on Tuesday night that she could barely think of anything else. Would Holy Cross give her a warning or expel her for cheating? Should we make plane reservations to go up and get her, just in case? Finally, Wednesday came. We asked Cait to call us immediately after class, and she did. She said when she entered the classroom she was shaking and almost frozen with fear of her future at Holy Cross. Her professor had her paper in his hand. It looked bad! He then simply asked her if he could disseminate her paper to all of her classmates as an example of how to write a great research paper. Cait was not expelled from school. In fact, she aced this particular class and went on to make the Dean's List that semester.

We had all gotten way ahead of ourselves. We were so focused on the fear of what the future might bring that we just couldn't think clearly. We were literally unable to live in the present out of fear for the future. The outcome was such a relief to all three of us, but we saw that we had all suffered needlessly—and at our own hand. It was a self-inflicted wound which could have been avoided had we realized we were worried about the future when we should have just taken a deep breath, realized that there was nothing we could do until Wednesday, and lived in the present until we had an answer. Sound familiar?

5

SYNCING BODY AND MIND

The mind messes up more shots than the body.

—Tommy Bolt

THE SUBCONSCIOUS MIND

According to Webster's dictionary, the subconscious mind is defined as the mental activities just below the threshold of consciousness. According to Vaishnavi Nagaraj, author of "Ten Ways to Activate Your Subconscious Mind to Get What You Want," the role of the subconscious is to follow your directives, generally in the form of repeated thoughts, messages, and communication. In this way, the subconscious mind can be controlled to aid the process of actually making things happen in the physical world in the form of manifestation. Your thoughts, communication, and messages take the form of a kind of intangible energy, which is converted by the subconscious mind into a tangible reality.

Most psychologists recognize both the conscious mind and the subconscious mind—that they can and do work hand in hand to accomplish a given task. While there is some debate on the subject of syncing mind and body in the field of psychology, I am in the camp that believes the mind and body not only *can* be synched, but *must* be synced for optimum performance. Using the subconscious mind effectively is an excellent method for syncing up mind and body.

The conscious mind is your personality. It's your thoughts and who you are as a person. But the subconscious mind lies just below the surface, unseen and unnoticed. It has no opinions, no thoughts of its own. It does not analyze or think. It processes and stores the information that the conscious mind feeds it. Your subconscious mind has what is called a homeostatic impulse. It keeps your body temperature at 98.6 degrees Fahrenheit. It keeps you breathing regularly and keeps your heart beating at a certain rate. Through your autonomic nervous system, it maintains a balance among the hundreds of chemicals within your billions of cells. It works automatically, seamlessly with the conscious mind by following its orders. It is a goal-oriented machine that does not differentiate between positive and negative feedback. It sees the picture the conscious mind develops, and it goes about accomplishing the action that matches up with that visual. That's why you've heard that visualization before a shot is so important. You are setting the table for your subconscious to take the wheel during the swing.

CATCH THE BALL

When someone throws a ball toward you, the conscious mind is aware that a spherical object is headed your way. In anticipation of the ball's arrival, the subconscious mind kicks into high gear. It makes an immediate calculation as to exactly when and exactly where the ball will arrive in your space. As it calculates, your arm has already begun to move towards the expected rendezvous point. Your fingers have started to open to allow the ball to impact the palm of your hand and clamp down on it upon arrival. Your conscious mind is aware of the action of catching the ball, but it takes a temporary backseat to get out of the way of the subconscious mind's actions. When the ball is thrown in your direction, you don't consciously say to yourself, *Move arm, open fingers, shift weight*, and so forth. It's automatic. You just do it.

Think of the third baseman in baseball getting a line drive hit head high, traveling directly at them at 100 miles an hour. The reaction is split second and handled by the subconscious mind. The ball seems to be in their glove simultaneously with the crack of the bat. Once the ball is in their glove, the conscious mind jumps back in and decides the next action, maybe a throw over to first base to get the runner out. If the throw is made to first base, it's the subconscious mind coordinating the drawback of the arm, the calculation of the angle of ball release, weight shift to lead foot, and so on.

In the golf swing, it's the subconscious mind's job to coordinate the supremely complicated motion of the golf swing. Here's what it might sound like in your head if the conscious mind were to be in charge of your swing:

> *Okay, move arms back while beginning to set the wrist angle, begin to move weight to right foot, turn shoulders, now turn hips, gently begin to let left knee break right, head steady, check spine angle, left shoulder under chin, wrists now at full cock, club at three inches under parallel, adjust grip pressure in left hand to lighter tension, now begin to move weight to left foot, start weight transfer off of right side, begin to move arms on downswing, begin to post left leg, gently begin to uncock wrists, start hip unwind, unwind shoulders further, maintain angle in wrists for now, continue to move weight into left foot, straighten left leg a bit more for final post, increase grip pressure in right hand, increase ten percent at impact, continue to move weight to left side, recheck spine angle, continue to move right knee, right knee toward target, keep head down at impact but prepare for it to move up*

and left with right shoulder, now fully extend arms at impact for maximum extension, turn shoulders past hips, check spine angle one more time, now fully post left leg straight, move weight to left side ninety percent, begin to lift right heel off the ground, rotate hips to maximum now to face target, accelerate arms past left shoulder, continue to move left heel off the ground and put eighty-five percent of weight on the outside of your left foot, and finish.

SEE IT, FEEL IT

As you can see, the golf swing is no job for the conscious mind. The swing must be powered by the subconscious mind, reacting to the image created by the conscious mind. But the conscious mind doesn't always know that. It can get in the way of the subconscious machine that is trying to make a golf swing. Scientists, including Dr. Maxwell Maltz in his book *Psycho-Cybernetics*, have proven that there are many ways your brain and nervous system operate as a machine. Although Dr. Maltz is clear in saying that you are not actually a machine, he makes numerous analyses that show how the brain and nervous system are machine-like in their operation. He calls them "servo-mechanisms."

For example, a golfer steps up to a par four with water all down the right side, and the conscious mind says, *Do not hit it right*! Because the subconscious mind processes and acts on both positive and negative thoughts equally, with no distinction between the two, it will see the water hazard but not be capable of making a judgement as to whether it is to be avoided or embraced. Thus, it may direct a swing that hits the ball into the hazard. We have all experienced hitting our shot directly at the hazard we had wished to avoid.

The other issue we have all experienced when body and mind are out of sync is when the conscious mind messes up an otherwise good swing because it refuses to step back long enough for the subconscious mind to make the swing. In the above example with the water on the right, the conscious mind makes sure to yank the tee ball into the trees on the left to avoid the water.

SCAR TISSUE

Scar tissue is the fibrous tissue that forms when normal tissue is destroyed by disease, injury, or surgery. Scar tissue forms when a wound heals after a cut, sore, burn, or other skin condition, or when an incision is made into the skin during surgery. But there is another sort of scar tissue that every golfer is far too familiar with: the mental sort. It comes in two basic forms.

Locational Scar Tissue

This happens when a particular golf hole always has your number. You seem to usually hit a good drive in the fairway, but then dump it in the water on your way to a double bogey (or worse). As this scenario happens repeatedly over time, scar tissue forms on your psyche. Even though it's the 15th hole, you start thinking about how many golf balls you have rinsed in that damn lake while playing the 1st hole. You make the turn, and you see lake fronting the green of 15. And God help you when you step up to the actual 15th tee box. You're already toast!

Clearly you are in a results-oriented mindset—nowhere in the present. But you can't help it—you have too much scar tissue! Well, you *can* help it. Unlike the traditional form of scar tissue formed by a physical scar, it is possible to chip away and actually reduce your locational scar tissue. Try this:

- Get in the present and focus solely on your process. The swing you are about to take on your scar-tissue hole is no different from hitting the same club on the driving range during warm-up. Do your best to work your pre-shot routine, work your process, and do not think in terms of the result.

- Shake things up. In the example of a hole with water fronting the green, hit a different club off the tee that will give you a different distance into the green. This can mean hitting more club off the tee even though it might be taking a greater risk on the tee shot than normal to give you a more manageable second shot distance.

Situational Scar Tissue

This one is thornier but can also be resolved. Situational scar tissue is when we have our round right where we want it, and it suddenly blows up for reasons unknown. For example, you have it three under par on the front nine and think, *Man, if I can just par out, I'd shoot a 69 and that would be a great score*! As in locational scar tissue, the cause of situational scar tissue is getting ahead of ourselves, focusing on results instead of staying in the present and working our process. As you might expect, the solution is to insulate your thoughts from results-oriented thinking. But there is more to it, and it may not make sense at first glance.

To defeat situational scar tissue, you have to suffer multiple times from what has caused this scar tissue to begin to build in the first place. I think you need to build up a bit *more* of this scar tissue. You have to have "been there, done that" enough to get sick of it. You have endured multiple disappointments and now you're just tired of it. At this point, you are forced to take a "whatever happens, happens" attitude and just let go of it. When you reach this point, you can return to the present by releasing the worry surrounding the result. *Voilà*!

Life Hack

It's tricky business to get out of our own way because it's only natural to overthink matters in an effort to get the best result. But more often than not, overthinking delivers a disappointing result. When we finally succeed in getting out of our own way, staying in that moment remains a struggle for most.

Case in point: I grew up with a swimming pool in my backyard and spent a large part of my day swimming and diving with the neighborhood kids. Boys being boys, we were always pushing each other to outperform one another by the tactful use of dares. I dare you to hold your breath for two minutes. Or I dare you to do a backflip from the diving board. Holding my breath was no big deal—but the backflip, or the "one-and-a-half gainer," as it was known, was my nemesis. The "one-and-a-half" refers to standing on the very edge of the diving board with one's back to the water, throwing the legs up over the head and rotating one and a half times to dive into the water headfirst.

I spent many punishing hours entering the water either under-rotated or over-rotated. Each created a painful smash of unprotected flesh hitting the water flat with a loud flopping sound. In every unsuccessful dive, it was my conscious mind going into panic mode as it recalled the pain of a prior unsuccessful dive. This caused my body to panic, too, and I lost any semblance of control or natural athleticism. I needed to find a way to simply feel where I was in space as I rotated through the air, not to think about where my body was.

I finally started to have some success in getting out of my own way by wearing a wet suit on my upper body that would cushion the water flop. With the promise of less pain on a poor dive, my mind slowly began to step back and let my subconscious mind take over the dive. I began to feel where my body was in space as I left the diving board, not think about where I was. Soon I was able to take off the wet suit and dive with no fear.

The best way to sync up body and mind is to figure out exactly what is causing your conscious mind to butt in and try to run things. In my diving, it was fear of flopping flat on the surface of the water and the associated pain (and embarrassment) that followed. In golf, or in almost anything else that is important to you, there is some reason that your mind is too active. Fear of failure (choking) is a common reason your conscious mind won't let go. But it can be other factors, too.

By getting to the matter of what is causing your conscious mind to be too involved in the process, you will find a way to neutralize it—calm it down. Focusing on the positive thoughts and choosing to ignore the negative thoughts is a good start. In my case, reminding myself that there are so many good things in my life to be thankful for gives me the perspective to focus on what is really important to me: my health, family, or friends. Doing so prompts me to remember that no one golf swing or business presentation will ever be the number-one most important event in my life. When I do that, I'm free to perform my best.

When you solve the puzzle of why your conscious mind
is too active, you will perform your best, too.

6

THE PRE-SHOT ROUTINE

Give me six hours to chop down a tree and
I will spend the first four sharpening the axe.
—Abraham Lincoln

ORDER AND CHAOS

Understand this: There is both chaos and order in tournament play. Order is all things within the light of the campfire. They are seen. Chaos, on the other hand, is unknown and beyond the light of the campfire. As the Taoist symbol of yin and yang suggests, order and chaos exist in the same space. The black paisley represents chaos and has a small white dot in it and the white paisley, representing order, has a black dot in it. The reason for these different color dots is that Taoists recognize that order can turn to chaos at any moment and that order can arise from chaos.

Wherever you go, whoever you are, your environment is composed of things you understand that act as expected and things which you do not understand that can knock you on your butt without warning. For the Tournament Golfer, this is as good an explanation of tournament golf as any. Order is established within the pre-shot routine and is a critical tool for the Tournament Golfer.

FINDING YOUR PRE-SHOT ROUTINE

The pre-shot routine is the structure within which the Tournament Golfer operates. It is their house—their shelter in the storm. This is the structure where a player's process begins. Pre-shot routines come in all shapes and sizes. They are individual to the player. There should be one for full swings and pitching as well as a separate and unique one for putting.

After you have analyzed the wind, lie quality, shot shape you need, where you are with your swing that day, and so on, select the club that best matches up with what the circumstances require. Your pre-shot routine begins when you pull the club out of the bag. It's a good idea to stand behind the ball and visualize the shot shape heading to your selected target. After that, it's up to you.

My pre-shot routine

Once I have evaluated the situation, and the club, and the type of shot best suited for that situation, I pull the club. My process begins now.

- I stand behind the ball, pick a spot about ten yards in front of me that is an intermediate target between my ball and the target.
- I take a full practice swing from behind the ball.
- I visualize the trajectory of my ball and the feel I'm going to have in my hands at contact.
- I step astride the ball and put my club behind the ball.
- I take a breath—in through my nose, out through my mouth.
- I take my stance.
- I look at my target.

- I look at my intermediate target.
- I look at the ball and take the club back.

A FAMILIAR FRIEND

A consistent pre-shot routine is central to the Tournament Golfer. When the heat is really on and the situation you find yourself in has the pressure dialed up, the genuine strength of the pre-shot routine is its *familiarity*. Stressful conditions in a tournament come in many forms. In a sense, situational pressure in a tournament is always the same, yet always a bit different. It's the same in that things seem to move a bit faster, your breath may get unsteady, and your mind may race; but it's also different because you are often on a different golf course, a different hole, under different weather conditions, and all the rest.

The pressure you're feeling is familiar—you have felt it many times before. And under pressure, golf becomes even lonelier than usual. There is no one there to hit the shot for you. You must execute your planned shot. It is your pre-shot routine that keeps you in that familiar place: in the present.

YOU'RE NOT ALONE

In the summer of 1985, I was playing in a U.S. Amateur qualifier. The last hole was a straightaway par four with water fronting the green, and I was in great shape to punch my ticket to the Am. I hit a solid drive in the fairway and from the tee, I breathed a sigh of relief as I saw the ball head down the line I intended. When I arrived at the ball's location, I was horrified to see that it was in a deep divot. The fairways were tight and firm, so I could see that the four walls of the divot were well defined and rigid. This type of divot made it difficult to predict ball flight coming out. Over half the ball was below ground level. I was 150 yards out, and I had to carry a water hazard (now called a "penalty area"). This was really bad timing for my ball to find a divot.

Things started to speed up. I heard myself explaining my bad luck of finding my ball in a divot on the last hole of the U.S. Am qualifier to my friends. They all had pained looks on their faces. One was patting me on the back and telling me that this was the worst break he had ever heard. I recognized that I had to find a way back to the matter at hand—to my next shot. Immediately, I began to count breaths. One, two. . . .

It was my turn. One of my playing partners had just spun his ball off the green and into the lake short of the green. This was not a good visual for me, and I put it out of my mind as best I could. It was in this moment that I learned the value of the design and execution of my pre-shot routine. I was about to find out if the hard work in designing and perfecting my unique pre-shot routine was worth it. The last thing a player does just prior to initiating step one of their pre-shot routine is to evaluate the situation and pull a club.

I decided that because the fairways were firm at ground level, the bottom of this divot was likely to be even firmer. The interior wall of the divot looked hard and crusty. Still, I was fortunate that the ball was situated near the center of the six-inch-long divot, instead of at one end or the other. I wondered if the player who'd made such a large, deep divot from 150 out chunked it in the lake. Most likely. *Forget it. Doesn't matter*, I thought. *Who cares?* With the bottom of the divot expected to be hard, I would need to make a steep descent to prevent the bottom of the club from bouncing into the ball, causing it to take off too low to carry the water.

The lake fronting the green was like an unexploded bomb, just waiting to blow up my entire round. I began my pre-shot routine and felt myself go into autopilot. Putting the ball back in my stance to steepen my downswing, I took the club back and let my subconscious mind take the wheel. The ball came out better than expected and checked up fifteen feet from the hole. *What a relief.* I 2-putted from there and snagged a spot in the Am.

It was my well-rehearsed pre-shot routine and the counting of my breaths that got me through the divot crisis. The breath pulled me back to the present (more on breathing in the next chapter), and the execution of the steps of my pre-shot routine enabled me to be process-oriented. By the time I implemented my pre-shot routine and I was ready to pull the trigger, I wasn't anxious about the water anymore. I was synced up and ready to hit the shot I needed.

A BREAK IN THE ROUTINE

The next time you watch a tour player on TV, study the pre-shot routine. I guarantee you will see it repeat over and over again like a carbon copy. Those times you see a player deviate from the pre-shot routine, you may see disaster. In 1970, Doug Sanders had a three-foot putt for par on the famous 18th hole at St. Andrews to win the Open. Go to YouTube and watch the video. He takes a brief look at the putt from behind and studies it from the other side of the hole. He steps over the putt confidently and places the putter behind the ball. There was no practice stroke, as was part of his pre-shot routine. He is all set to go and about to make a short putt to win the Open.

What many people don't remember is that Doug's short putt was for a 2-putt that started from about twenty-five feet above the hole. When over the twenty-five-footer, he's about to make the stroke and hears something that distracts him, taking him away from the task at hand. He immediately straightens up and correctly pulls himself off the ball to start his pre-shot routine over from the beginning. He does so and hits a decent first putt to about three feet. The now famous three-footer.

While over the remaining three-foot putt left for the win, he breaks his pre-shot routine when he bends down and removes a loose impediment from his line while still over the putt. Unlike the prior putt, when a random sound caused Doug to restart his pre-shot routine, he inexplicably stays in place on this putt, deciding not to start things over.

Doug typically stood over putts longer than most—about twelve seconds. By deviating from his pre-shot routine, however, he was over the ball a full twenty-eight seconds—an eternity. Had he stepped off the three-footer and restarted, it would have enabled him to return to his process, safe inside the shelter of his pre-shot routine and ready to make the putt. Instead, he was out on a ledge with an extra sixteen seconds to think of all the ways he could miss this putt.

As we all know, Doug Sanders missed that putt, which placed him in a tie with Jack Nicklaus. The next day the two squared off for the first 18-hole playoff in Open history. Doug gave Jack a great match but came up one shot short. Nicklaus nearly drove the 18th green, chipping it to three feet and making birdie to win the playoff by one stroke. The video of Sanders missing his second putt on 18 isn't the only memorable scene from that hole for this Open. Nicklaus is seen flinging his putter in the air above his head in celebration of making his birdie to win the Open at St. Andrews.

Nicklaus would later say, "If you're going to be a player that people remember, you have to win the Open at St. Andrews." In this case, both winner and loser will forever have their place in history. Sanders would say thirty years after his famous miss, "It doesn't hurt much anymore. These days I can go a full five minutes without thinking about it." Doug lived in Houston, and we saw a lot of each other over the years. When he spoke of the ill-fated stroke that day on the 72nd hole at St. Andrews, he would do his best to laugh it off. But that laugh always sounded a little different, a little off-key. There was no doubt the damage of that missed putt cut deep into his soul.

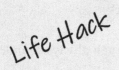

Life Hack

Develop a routine for all things in your life. At my firm, Financial Synergies, we teach our advisors that the best way to maintain control of the context of a meeting is by having a thought-out plan in advance—a framework to use so that the meeting has a better chance of being a successful one. Much like the pre-shot routine in golf, we have a predetermined list of actions which need to be executed before a client meeting. For example, we review notes from prior meetings so that any outstanding client requests or concerns can be further addressed. Isn't this like the golf swing? Don't we want to have all of our pre-shot doubts or prior issues dealt with before we step up to the ball?

If you want consistent results in your work, your golf, or your life, develop the pre-shot routine to increase your odds of a successful outcome

7

THE BREATH

If you want to conquer the anxiety of life,
live in the moment, live in the breath.

—Amit Ray

AN ANCHOR TO THE PRESENT MOMENT

The breath is a point of concentration. By focusing on the breath, you become aware of the mind's inclination to wander into the past or the future. The simple discipline of the breath brings us back to the present moment along with the concentration and clarity of mind it provides. In Buddhism, this training of the mind is called *dhyāna*. The breath is a good antidote to impatience and anxiety, and a most effective way to relax. The breath anchors us to the present moment.

We tend to experience everything in our lives with our head. The breath encourages us to let go of our thinking briefly and focus on the belly. We feel the consistency of the breath, its rising and falling, and the physical sensations of movement that complement it. The breath allows us to synchronize body and mind. When we feel the breath, we feel the confirmation of being alive. Even under the most stressful conditions, the breath cleanses us.

We are not completely in charge of our breathing. We can hold our breath for a time, but fairly soon any attempt to hold the breath too long will produce countermeasures from within.

It's possible to learn to align with the breath, gently moving with it, while allowing an opening for it to come into its own comfortable depth and tempo. Things seem to go best when we cooperate with the breath, rather than resisting it. In a very real sense, this dance with the breath reminds us that, like life, we have only partial control.

THE BREATH IS YOUR COMPANION

In 2020, a disc in my back collapsed and pinched the adjacent nerve controlling my right leg. The pain was indescribable, and I would need back surgery to save the nerve and my leg. The ten days between onset and surgery were incredibly challenging. Nerve pain is impervious to all pain medications, which meant I had to find a way to endure the pain without the benefit of narcotics. The pain was relentless, and I lost fifteen pounds in the days running up to my surgery, as it wouldn't allow me to eat.

I was able to sleep for only thirty minutes at a time before a new pain wave would strike, thrusting a knife into my thigh. When a new round of pain showed up, I began to count my breaths. The breath took some of the edge off the torment. At night, the breath gave me hope. It was the breath, and my wife, Pat, that got me through this most difficult time.

In tournament play, counting breaths is the most effective way to pull yourself back into the present when your mind has wandered back into results-oriented golf. When you're feeling situational pressure on the course, there is nothing like breathing to make you self-aware and to bring you back to the present moment. Deep breathing activates the parasympathetic nervous system, which is the body's "rest and digest" system. When the parasympathetic nervous system is activated, your heart rate and blood pressure lower.

Start by being aware of your breath—nothing else. A *breath cycle* is an inhale plus an exhale and should last about eight seconds, total. Breathe in through your nose deeply and out through your mouth. Count "one" on each exhale. See if you can count through five breath cycles without thinking of anything else. It isn't easy. It takes practice. Do it on the green while waiting for your turn to putt or when walking between shots.

AM I BREATHING?

In 1977, I was in North Carolina at Pinehurst Number Four. I was at my first tour school. I made the cut and went into the back nine of the final round feeling confident that I was inside the golden qualifying bubble of the top twenty-five—those players who would earn a tour card to play the PGA Tour the following year. I was doing a decent job of staying in the present, working my process.

I stood on the tee box of the 72nd hole and hit a solid drive in the center of the fairway of this long par four finishing hole. I had a 5 iron into the green, hit it pretty solid, but I tugged it a bit into the front, greenside bunker. *No big deal*, I thought. Good lie. I stepped confidently into the bunker and thought, *Even if I don't get this up and down, I'm going to qualify; I'm going to be a tour player!* I then bladed the shot over the green and into the back bunker. And that's not all. My ball found a downhill lie in that bunker. Things started to accelerate, and my mind began to race uncontrollably. I was no longer in the present, and all thoughts of process swiftly departed.

What am I going to tell everyone back home? Doubling the last hole to miss my tour card by one? What a choker I am! What am I going to do for the next year? (Tour schools were held once a year). I instinctively began to count my breaths. *In, out one. In, out two.* I can't say I got totally present by counting those breaths, but I was definitely back in North Carolina at Pinehurst Number Four! I pulled out some solid positive self-talk, surrendered to the outcome, and prepared to hit my second bunker shot on the same damn hole.

I had to clip it pretty well to put some spin on it and barely carry the lip of the bunker because it was all downhill to the pin, and looked like it could run out. The downhill lie wasn't going to help things, either. I pulled the shot off, hitting it close enough to salvage bogey and learn a very big lesson. *Work my process. Stay in the present.* I got my tour card by one shot.

Life Hack

In this modern life, we are constantly under some sort of stress. The breath can do much for lowering that stress. Studies back this up. In two studies conducted at The University of Arizona and Yale involving veterans from Iraq and Afghanistan who struggled with trauma, breathing exercises dramatically reduced their anxiety levels after just one week. They also continued to experience the mental health benefits a full year later. Another study split participants into two groups. One group used the technique of conventional cognitive strategies for stress management to intellectually figure out why a participant was stressed. The second test group used breathing. The second group exhibited immediate lessening of stress through breathing and measurable improvement of mood, which remained increased when measured months later.

When we are in a highly stressed state, our prefrontal cortex, where our rational thought resides, becomes impaired. We have all experienced this. When under stress, we don't make our best decisions. Sometimes, we find ourselves unable to make a decision at all. With the breath comes the return of logical thinking. Changing the rhythm of your breath lowers your heart rate and signals your body to begin to relax. When you experience delight, your breathing is usually deep and slow. When you feel anxious or fearful, your breathing becomes shallow, fast, and irregular. Research indicates that emotions are tied to our breath, so changing the breath can change how we feel. When you initiate a breathing pattern, you feel the emotion associated with that pattern.

To get a sense of how the breath can calm you down, try changing the ratio between inhaling vs. exhaling. When you inhale, your heart rate speeds up. When you exhale, it slows down. Breathe in for a count of three and out for a count of six for a few minutes to calm your nervous system down. If you still feel some anxiety, lengthen the time spent on the exhales.

Using breathing in all elements of your life will lead to less anxiety and help you deal with the stress of modern life.

8

WHAT YOU CAN CONTROL
AND WHAT YOU CANNOT

The more we are concerned with the things we cannot control,
the less we will do with the things we can control.

—John Wooden

RELINQUISHING CONTROL

Much of the frustration of life is trying to differentiate between things we can control and those that we cannot. The reality is, there are many things in life that we cannot control. People who resist this truth become control freaks. They think if they can somehow control a situation, they can prevent bad things from happening. Nowhere is this frustration more applicable than on the golf course.

The problem with worrying about things you cannot control is that it wears you down, hindering you from working effectively on those things over which you *do* have control. Focus on those things you can control and prepare yourself for the events that you have no control over. Remember, many of the events we have no control over are *pleasant*.

To be a Tournament Golfer, you can't worry about what others think. As I mentioned in my introduction, tournament golf exposes players to a wider range of people and accompanying criticism. Every tournament score you post gets reviewed by someone. Golf is humbling. Embrace it. No one will know anything about you 100 years from now anyway.

WHAT YOU CAN CONTROL
Three things you can control

1. **Your mindset:** You are in control of your mindset because your mindset is an inside job. Clearly, your mindset is likewise impacted by external events, which are out of your control. So, mindset is established not so much from the external circumstances you find yourself in, but how you interpret and respond to them. How you think about something is ultimately how you will feel about it.

2. **Your effort:** Make an effort to stay positive. There is always something we learn from a bad experience. It may not be clear at the time, but there is always a lesson to be discovered. It is an accepted belief that we learn more from failure than success. Life is a journey at any age, so it essential to continue to grow and learn.

3. **Your behavior:** How will you respond? Ninety-five percent of life isn't what happens to us but how we respond to it. What is your behavior when your ball is ten feet from the hole but buried in the lip of the greenside bunker? Are you going to throw a club in anger? Or knuckle down, accept the situation, and focus on the challenge presented? Ultimately, the only thing you have much control over is *you*.

STICK TO YOUR KNITTING

In 1963, at Royal Lytham & St. Annes, a young Jack Nicklaus was about to win his first Open. He teed off on 17 with what he thought was a two-stroke lead over Bob Charles and Phil

Rodgers who were paired together in the group behind him. As Jack describes it, "I had 212 in for my second shot and the pin was tucked way back in the left-hand corner. I told my caddie, Jimmy Dickenson, 'Give me the 2-iron.' Jimmy said to hit 3-iron because there was no need to get it all the way back there. I had listened for any applause from 16 green and didn't hear a sound. I assumed that neither Bob nor Phil had made a birdie, so I was still up by two. But the wind had prevented me from hearing the applause—*both* players made birdie."

Nicklaus hit the 2-iron in what was later described as an un-necessarily aggressive play. His ball went long into some gnarly rough over the green, and Jack barely got it on the green making bogey. On the 18 tee box, Nicklaus thought he carried a one-shot lead but he was actually tied with Charles and Rodgers. He played 18 too conservatively, settling for bogey from the rough. Bob Charles would be the champion that year, winning his only major championship. Nicklaus would later say, "How stupid could I be?"

Jack Nicklaus recognized he should have played his own game and waited until play was finished to see how things turned out. He had no control over what was going on in the group behind him, yet he allowed what he thought they were doing to influence his current play. He vowed never to make that mistake again.

Most everything else is not 100 percent under our control. We cannot control the weather. We cannot control what others think. We sure cannot control the past—although some will try, with their explanations. We cannot control the future, either. The Tournament Golfer understands the difference between what they can control and what they cannot. If you enter a tournament and do a poor job of controlling your mindset—not giving each swing your best effort, or behaving badly—you will have regrets.

The past is past. You have a degree of control over your future, even though much is unknown. Not the past. When it is done, you no longer have control over it. We all have regrets and we've all made mistakes. The best we can do is to make decisions as to how our past acts will affect our future. This knowledge comes from learning from our mistakes to avoid repeating them.

We build on our triumphs to boost our confidence and enhance our chances of repeating them.

Marcus Aurelius wisely declared, "You have power over your mind—not outside events. Realize this, and you will find strength."

Life Hack

A good rule for life is to always be willing to learn. We learn from things we have some control over—which are usually mistakes we have made. We also learn from things we have no control over, which are usually circumstances thrust upon us.

An example of messing up a situation we had some control over would be hitting a ball in a lake because we decided to take an aggressive line off the tee. Learning this painful lesson allows us to be less aggressive next time.

But those events we have no control over, such as getting rear-ended while sitting in our car at a traffic light, are not so easy. *I didn't do anything wrong! I was just sitting in my car!* It's human nature to start to think of ourselves as a victim. But victimhood is like a cancer. If it isn't caught early and dealt with, it will spread throughout every corner of our lives. It causes us to perpetually feel sorry for ourselves. Once you're convinced that you're a victim, you can find yourself in a destructive tailspin that paints everything black. It becomes a dark, self-fulfilling prophesy. As soon as you surrender to victimhood's call, you surrender control of your life to an outside agency.

Evaluate what has happened; take a minute to regret that it happened; then see about making the best of it. Don't let victimhood take root in your mind. You are not a victim unless you decide to become a victim.

9
TAKING RESPONSIBILITY

*The moment you take responsibility for everything in your life is
the moment you can change anything in your life.*

—Hal Elrod

YOU ARE RESPONSIBLE

Avoiding the stress of worrying about what you cannot control
is important—but taking responsibility for those things over
which you *do* have control is just as important. There are few
matters more important on the course and in life than taking
responsibility. As a golfing friend of mine once told me on this
subject, "Don't explain, don't complain." What he meant was,
don't make excuses—and quit whining about the cruelty of
golf.

Taking responsibility for ourselves achieves wonders.

Being accountable for our actions is also linked to self-esteem.
People who make no excuses are appreciated by those around
them. They are viewed as credible. Have you ever heard someone
say, "Wow, Mary is so amazing. She always has an excuse." No,
you've never heard that. No one likes a whiner or an excuse-
maker. People who take responsibility for their actions are held
in high regard. More importantly, being responsible sets one free.
When a person is accountable for what happens to them, no one
can control them. They cease being a victim.

WITH ACCOUNTABILITY COMES CLARITY.

By taking personal responsibility, Tournament Golfers have the opportunity to reflect on why they had a bad day on the course, and to develop a strategy to avoid the issues that made for that bad day. There are three primary components of taking responsibility, which all Tournament Golfers possess:

1. **Honesty:** Being honest about their failures on the course that led to poor results is the most effective path toward fixing a problem. The Tournament Golfer gives an honest accounting of the trouble so that it can be addressed and not repeated. The Golfer-Who-Plays-Tournaments will often lie to themselves to avoid the pain—which does not address the issue in the least. Without honesty, they are doomed to repeat their mistakes.

2. **Fairness:** Tournament Golfers seek fairness for themselves. They accept responsibility while understanding that blaming themselves for those things that were out of their control is destructive. They also make sure not to hang onto the memory of poor performances. No good friend would ever remind us of our lousy tournament performance, so why would we do it to ourselves? Be your own best friend.

3. **Courage:** Courage could be defined as having strength in the face of fear or pain. Tournament Golfers have the courage to give an honest assessment of their situation so they can come up with solutions. A great example is the post-round debrief. This means going through the mistakes made

during a round and identifying their origins. This process takes courage and deep self-reflection. It can be as simple as recognizing a part of your game that needs more practice, or isolating technical flaws that are causing issues which your teacher can pinpoint. Or, it can be a thought process that leads to an understanding of how you took a bad swing or made a poor decision.

Winston Churchill said, "Responsibility is the price of greatness." Be great. Take responsibility.

Life Hack

At my firm, we help people make important financial decisions which come up in life. We also manage over one billion dollars of clients' money. In dealing with clients, communication is critical to avoid making mistakes. But mistakes can, and will, happen. At our firm, we teach all team members to take responsibility for their mistakes. When an error has occurred, we must do the own it, fix it, and eliminate it.

Own it: Everyone makes mistakes. Human error is a term we are all too familiar with. Mistakes are what define the human condition. So, when a mistake is made, even if it isn't black and white as to who was at fault, we take possession of it. The first act after owning a mistake is to make it known that we now own it and that an apology must take place. Being defensive about who poorly communicated—the client or the team member—is a fool's errand. Why be "right" if it runs a client off? No matter what, a client will not appreciate their advisor blaming them for the error, even if it is clearly the client's mistake.

Fix it: This might sound obvious but taking responsibility for a blunder is not quite taking full responsibility. The misstep must now be fixed. The fix can be an uncomplicated, easy one, or it can be a costly time-consuming one. Either way, it must be dealt with ASAP. Drop everything else and rectify the issue.

Eliminate it: To be honest, it's more of a sincere *promise* to eliminate the mistake. We explain to the client why it will never happen again, and then make sure the slip-up isn't repeated. But we are human. It could happen again, and therefore we must work hard to avoid a recurrence.

Accepting responsibility is easily the most important attribute a firm like mine can have. It promotes healthy interaction between us and our clients. It is a badge of honor because it is our duty to take responsibility for a mistake. This philosophy of handling mistakes is deeply ingrained in our corporate culture. Because it is elemental to our culture, no one need be afraid of being chastised for mistakes made in the future. It is an honest acceptance of the fact that to be human is to make mistakes.

Try this in your daily life: Accept that you are human and take responsibility for negative outcomes—even if you feel an outcome is not your fault. Taking responsibility is liberating. First of all, it disarms most people. People feel that when a mistake is made against them, they are the victim, and they are willing to fight to certify their victimhood. I say, certify it for them. Secondly, you may be surprised at the immense relief you feel because assuming responsibility is the definition of taking control.

No one can pull your chain or beat you up—because when you take responsibility, you win. You preserve the relationship with your friend, client, or family member. They can no longer command you.

THE TOURNAMENT GOLFER. . .

USGA "Medalist" Medals

Duke Butler and me
1985

Tiger and me
1992

National Champions
University of Houston Golf Team
1977

National Championship Ring
University of Houston
1977

*Jack Nicklaus presenting
inaugural course record plaque
Carlton Woods CC
2001*

*Golf Trophies
2002*

*Texas Senior Am
Player of the Year Presentation
2015*

Texas Senior Am
2015

Jackie Burke and me
2017

*Texas Golf Hall of Fame
Induction
2019*

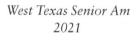

*West Texas Senior Am
2021*

10

EMBRACE THE SUCK

Sometimes we are tested not to show our weaknesses,
but to discover our strengths.

—Anonymous

ALLOW FOR ADVERSITY

More than just dealing with adversity as it comes, the Tournament Golfer takes it a step further. They embrace the suck, accepting the inherent tough breaks that tournament golf promises. No time is spent worrying about it or when it will show up. Our culture often says, "Don't be a victim," but Tournament Golfers know they became a victim the day they picked up a club. Allowing for adversity—even when its exact time of arrival and the form it will take are unknowns—is empowering. Surrendering to the outcome in advance makes the Tournament Golfer tough to defeat. It is mental toughness defined. And it can be your suit of armor.

THE COURSE

There are two common examples where the Tournament Golfer drastically outshines the Golfer-Who-Plays-Tournaments: 1. when the competition is held at a golf course they don't like and 2. inclement weather.

In my own experience, playing in Houston's City Amateur was a perfect example. The championship was held at the revered Memorial Park Golf course, a classic venue. The Houston area is known to have some of the best players in all of the country. To win the Houston City Am was a great honor—with the list of players on the trophy displaying a Who's Who of the greatest amateur players in Texas.

However, back in the eighties, Memorial Park was rarely in good shape. It wasn't anyone's fault that the old girl struggled to be in good shape. For starters, the irrigation system had not been updated since it opened in July of 1936. It was not an automatic system that could be controlled remotely. Maintenance crews had to find the sprinkler nozzle in the ground and manually screw the sprinkler head into the nozzle to water a particular area. This process meant that some areas would be incredibly lush, while a couple of yards away was hard pan or bare dirt. It was disheartening to rip a drive right down the middle and find your ball in a patch of high grass or dirt. It was easy to get down about it, feel sorry for yourself, and play the victim.

Needless to say, players could get terrible lies—nearly unplayable lies—even after hitting a good golf shot. It was maddening. I took the attitude that at least once per round, maybe more, I was going to get a really bad lie. But it was the same for everyone. By accepting this eventuality ahead of time, I had a huge advantage over the players who, post-round, would try to outdo each other over who had the worst break that day. Misery loves company, but I made a point of staying away from this particular company. Over the years, by embracing the suck of a course that could punish and often fail to reward a good golf shot, I was able to earn eight Houston City Amateurs, four Amateurs and four Senior Amateurs, all conducted on city courses.

I have never really cared about the state of the site for a competition or the venue itself. Don't get me wrong, I have thoroughly enjoyed playing events at some of the greatest golf courses in the world—The U.S. Am at Pebble Beach, the British Senior at

Royal County Down, and more. I know there are many Golf-ers-Who-Play-Tournaments who entered the event to get to play some great course hosting a championship. That's not me. I'm here to compete, and that's my overriding focus. And if the course is in poor shape, then my chances of winning have just improved dramatically.

THE WEATHER

Poor weather at an event is very different from a poor course or poor course conditions, because it is unrelenting and also random. For the most part, the weather is here to stay, and a player must deal with it on every shot, all day. The persistence of high wind, rain, or cold can wear a player down, make them give up and want to go home. This is your chance. If it's bad enough, some of the field will withdraw. The vast majority of the remaining players will have quit mentally even though they haven't technically withdrawn from the event. This leaves about ten percent of the field left for you to beat. I like those odds. Embrace the suck.

SUCKING AT SCHOOL

When I was a player on the University of Houston golf team, we were highly ranked and always the team to beat when we teed it up. In fact, the Golf Channel recently ran an episode mention-ing my 1977 team and concluded that our team was perhaps the best golf team the university had ever put together. That's saying something, as the University of Houston, through the golf pro-gram's sixteen national championships, holds the record for any division—one school, any sport. What we came to realize was that a fair bit of gamesmanship came with being a top-ranked team. For example, it was pretty typical for us to get super-ear-ly tee times—like 7:00 in the morning or even a touch earlier. When staying in a hotel and sharing a room, this meant that we would have to set our alarms for 4:30 or so and order breakfast the night before because, often, the restaurants close to our hotel didn't open until shortly before our tee time.

Now, there were guys on the team who really took offense to this particular tactic. I remember one prominent player saying, "We are the number-one ranked team in the tournament. We should get more respect!" I actually loved it. For me, this was solid confirmation that the other schools recognized we were the top dogs, and they would stoop to almost anything to tip the scales in their favor. It made winning tournaments that much sweeter when we overcame their weak attempts to throw us off our routine. I gladly embraced the suck with an even wider smile on my face when posing with the trophy!

Another opportunity to embrace the suck was the 1977 Southwest Conference Championship in Tyler, Texas. It was hosted by Southern Methodist University, and we were favored to win. I was paired with a player from SMU the first round, and I was having a lot of trouble reading the greens. I might read a putt to break a little left, and it was breaking right. Twice on the back nine after I missed a putt by a mile, I dropped my ball back down and tried the putt once again—just to see if it had broken the wrong way or if I had just missed stroking down my intended line. My practice putt was after my group had finished the hole, and confirming the group behind us wasn't ready to hit their approach shots so I wasn't slowing down the pace of play. Even with my less-than-stellar green reading, I went on to shoot a solid one under 71.

At the end of the round, when the SMU player who was keeping my score gave me my card to review, it said I shot 75. Now, anyone who plays in tournaments knows that scores kept by a person in your group can be off by a stroke, maybe two. But never by as much as four. I knew immediately that something was very wrong. He saw the look on my face and before I could say something, he said, "It's a two-stroke penalty to hit a practice putt—even after you have completed the hole."

I hadn't realized that I was playing in a tournament that issued a two-stroke penalty for hitting a practice putt, even after the player finished putting their original ball. This local rule was typically implemented to speed up play, the reasoning behind it being that if all players hit second putts to see what they did wrong on their first putt, it would slow down the pace.

Obviously, I protested, insisting he was wrong. In all tournaments you play, the Tournament Committee has final say on any rule controversies. Guess who was head of this tournament's Rules Committee? If you guessed the SMU golf coach, you would be right. He promptly confirmed that I had indeed violated the rules, and assessed me a four-stroke penalty—as I had made two practice putts on the back nine, each requiring a two-stroke penalty.

After about an hour of haggling, involving other players and coaches, it was determined that a two-stroke penalty for hitting a practice putt after the ball has been holed must be clearly stated on the rules sheet of the specific tournament. It wasn't. My 71 was reinstated. We went on to win the Southwest Conference Championship—with Ed Fiori, John Stark, and me finishing first, second, and third individually. It was a dominant performance.

Again, I recognized that the other teams—this time SMU—had so much respect for us, they would do just about anything to defeat us. But try as they might, using all the dirty tricks they could gather, they still came up short. This win was particularly gratifying because of the outrageous attempt by our opponents (players and coaches) to bend the rules or toss them out altogether, in order to win an event.

While the guys on my team were complaining about this incident weeks later, I embraced the suck enthusiastically.

DRAMA QUEENS

The Golfer-Who-Plays-Tournaments has a hard time processing this concept. When they lip-out a putt and it hangs on the edge, they become instant drama queens. Classic drama-queen gestures? They might contort their bodies and jerk around as if having a medical emergency of some sort. Often, they stay still as if frozen in place as they try to process their terrible misfortune, much like a soap opera actor at the end of a dramatic scene. They may stare in disbelief for a while as players in their threesome must wait until the show is over to hit their putts. Tournament Golfers immediately walk up, tap in and go about their business. To them, the lip-out is ancient history by the time they put their putter back in their bag. That's embracing the suck. You can do it, too.

One more thing about embracing the suck. When done well, it also intimidates the hell out of your opponents. Think about it: When you see your opponent get a truly terrible break on the course and then shake it off, isn't that pretty intimidating? They just got screwed by the golf gods, but they show zero reaction and keep moving forward! That's pretty terrifying! How are you ever going to beat them?

Life Hack

In *The Oz Principle* by Roger Conners, Tom Smith, and Craig Hickman, the book's authors describe people "languishing in the victim cycle [who] begin to lose their spirit and will until they eventually feel powers. If they choose to continue feeling victimized, they will move through an unending cycle that thwarts individual productivity."

Embracing the suck is accepting misfortune for what it is and not becoming a victim.

Psychologist Alia J. Crum, PhD, Principal Investigator for the Stanford Mind & Body Lab, has developed a three-step model for dealing with the suck in everyday life.

- **Step 1:** See it. See the stress. We don't stress about things that have little or no importance to us. When we acknowledge what we care about, solutions become more obvious. For example, on the days I am feeling stressed out, I ask my wife Pat, "Why the hell am I so stressed?" I'm not really looking for her to answer. I am looking to figure out what is really going on at the root cause of my anxiety. Often, what is causing the stress is something unrelated to what I first thought it was.

- **Step 2:** Own it. Owning the suck is the essence of embracing and welcoming it so that it can be overcome. If it is important to you, then it is what you have chosen to do. Make it work.

- **Step 3**: Use it. Stress about a certain situation will not kill us. The body's reaction to a stressful situation is designed to boost the mind and body into an augmented state. If it doesn't kill you, it will make you stronger.

The key to embracing the suck is not just to evade being victim. It is actually appreciating the suck so that it might empower you—strengthen you. Embracing the suck is not trying to avoid or ignore the pain of the moment, but rather, to come to terms with it by relishing the discomfort of the experience. One spectacular example of this is the physically disabled individual. To live as full a life as possible, they embrace the suck of their circumstances every day and find a way to make it work. They rise above their handicap by embracing it through acceptance. I have never met a handicapped adult, be they blind or wheelchair-bound, who didn't have a naturally positive outlook on life even though their day-to-day life is such a struggle.

They see it, own it, and use it.

11

SURROUND YOURSELF WITH GOLFERS WHO ARE BETTER THAN YOU

*Always surround yourself with people who are better than you.
If you're hanging around bad people, they're going to start
bringing you down. But if you surround yourself with good
people, they're going to be pulling you up.*

—Donny Osmond

GETTING YOUR BUTT KICKED

I was a member of a club, north of my hometown of Houston, which had in it a lot of single-handicap players in its membership. There was one particular group of players that had a regular game I frequently joined. They were some of the best players in the club, and I have always gravitated to playing with highly skilled golfers when I could because this helped me elevate my game. It made me better.

The best example I can think of isn't even golf, though. It's basketball. When my daughter Caitlin was eight, she played on a basketball team. I was one of the coaches. The organizers of the league asked if we would consider playing up in the nine-year-old division because there were too many teams in the eight-year-old division and too few in the nine-year-old division. The other coach and I discussed this for a few days and decided it would be a good experiment to do this for our girls, to hone their skills. We let the parents know our intentions and they were on board, too.

We went 0–8 and had a season of sustained grumbling from the girls. Most of them stepped up, doubled, and redoubled their efforts against the taller, stronger girls we went up against. Still, we consistently got our butts kicked by these older girls. The primary job of parents and coaches is to teach and encourage the players; but this season, it was especially important. The following year we played in our own age group—and to say we dominated the other nine-year-old teams is an understatement. We were undefeated! The game was typically already over by halftime. The thing I remember most was how tough our girls had become. Every player had improved by leaps and bounds. Having gone through the prior season of defeats, the girls had formed a closer bond. Encouraging each other had become a habit.

Whenever possible, Tournament Golfers seek out better players. They understand there is a great deal to be learned from them. Much of the knowledge picked up from playing with better players isn't what they say or even the quality of shots they hit. It's about how they manage their way around the golf course. Better players know their limitations and don't try shots that are unnecessary or foolish in a given situation. They know when to go for the pin and when to recognize a sucker pin when they see one. They know how to act.

POSITIVE GOLFERS

The people you hang out with have a huge impact on you. The people you play golf with have a huge impact on your golf game. Famously, Jim Rohn once said, "You're the average of the five people you spend most of your time with." If you surround yourself with negative people who constantly have drama and excuses attached to everything they do, especially their golf, some of that is bound to rub off on you. Don't play a practice round with someone who always complains about the course hosting the tournament. Before you know it, you'll start complaining about the course, too—and slowly you'll become a victim, chock-full of excuses.

It's easy for us to underestimate the importance of the company we keep. Most of us need people as mentors or good friends who tell us the truth about ourselves and help us up our game because of them. Surrounding ourselves with positive-thinking, successful people challenges us to be our best selves.

Life Hack

Andrew Carnegie, one of the most successful industrialists of all time, said, "Never be so foolish as not to surround yourself with people who are smarter than you." Carnegie shared this wisdom as one of his reasons for success. In my business life, I have endeavored to hire people with one or more skills surpassing my own. Like Carnegie, I know the best team is one possessing differing skillsets that not only complement each other but also help us arrive at the best solutions. This is the true definition of creating synergy. I named my company Financial Synergies with this fact in mind.

Henry Ford is credited with a similar quote. "I am not the smartest, but I surround myself with competent people." In fact, Ford was famously indignant when he was being questioned in a courtroom by an opposing lawyer. "If I should really *want* to answer the foolish question you have just asked, or any of the other questions you have been asking me, let me remind you that I have a row of electric push-buttons on my desk, and by pushing the right button, I can summon to my aid men who can answer *any* question I desire to ask concerning the business to which I am devoting most of my efforts. Now, will you kindly tell me, *why* I should clutter up my mind with general knowledge, for the purpose of being able to answer questions, when I have men around me who can supply any knowledge I require?" So, Ford didn't feel he had to have all the answers at the tip of his tongue. He surrounded himself with capable people.

There was a time in my life when I felt threatened by individuals who were smarter than I. Maybe it's because I've gotten older and meeting people smarter than I am has become more commonplace—but nowadays I really enjoy spending time with smart people. I appreciate hearing their take on things and gaining their perspective. I have benefitted by filling my home life as well as work life with really smart people. You can, too.

12

BE YOUR OWN BFF

*It's not what you say to everyone else that determines
your life. It's what you whisper to yourself
that has the greatest power.*

—Robert T. Kiyosoki

POSITIVE SELF-TALK

Tournament Golfers must be their own best friend. Golf is difficult and solitary, so it's essential to be positive to yourself to be an effective Tournament Golfer. It's okay to demand much of yourself and even to be disappointed in yourself from time to time. That's an inherent part of the game. Unlike most mainstream sports, there is no teammate to pick you up when things get tough. There's no one to cover for you—it's all on you.

Positive self-talk is crucial. Science backs up this claim: According to Dr. Mihaly Csikszentmihalyi in his book *Evolving Self: A Psychology for the Third Millennium,* "nothing can sap your belief in yourself or in your dreams more quickly and thoroughly than you, your own negative self-talk. For a variety of evolutionary reasons, the human mind automatically gravitates toward negative, frightening, and depressing thoughts."

DEFY THE DESTRUCTIVE VOICE

Pay attention to any negative self-talk going through your mind during a competitive round. It usually takes the form of the second person, as in *You are a terrible putter.* It's never *I am a terrible putter*. Golfers will allow their inner critic to speak to them in abusive ways they would never tolerate from anyone else. Learn to listen for negative self-talk when it pops up and recognize it for the lie that it is. Dr. Csikszentmihalyi refers to this negative self-talk as graffiti being sprayed on the walls of the mind. Immediately counter this negativity with a positive affirmation. Importantly, Dr. Csikszentmihalyi recommends countering the second-person criticism—*You* are a terrible putter—with a first-person affirmation: *I* am a *great* putter. The key is to learn to catch the negative self-talk and reverse it immediately and repeatedly.

Psycho-Cybernetics had a big influence on me in high school. The author, Dr. Maxwell Maltz, was a plastic surgeon. Through his practice, he discovered that people are who they believe themselves to be even if there is evidence to the contrary. For example, after a significant facial plastic surgery, many of his patients would see no change in their physical appearance. He theorized that although people are not conscious of it, their self-image develops because of their past experiences. A person tends to believe this self-image, and live their life based on this belief of themselves. This explains how some people seem to always be successful, and others constantly fail.

Their subsequent experiences will support the self-image they have of themselves. Interestingly, Maltz also discovered that negative self-images can be adjusted, tweaked, and even completely reversed through the use of the imagination—simply by picturing success. He believed that the conscious mind imagines the picture of a goal, and the subconscious mind goes about accomplishing that goal.

SHORT-TERM MEMORY LOSS

To truly become a Tournament Golfer, you must be able to conjure up a short-term memory loss on demand. A major difference between a Tournament Golfer and a Golfer-Who-Plays-Tournaments is the ability to move past a bad shot, a bad decision, or a bad situation—immediately after it occurs. It is not an exaggeration to say that virtually every time you play golf, things won't go your way for a variety of reasons.

Bobby Jones said, "On the golf course, a man may be the dogged victim of inexorable fate, be struck down by an appalling stroke of tragedy, become the hero of unbelievable melodrama, or the clown in a sidesplitting comedy—any of these within a few hours, and all without having to bury a corpse or repair a tangled personality."

There is just no getting around it: If you cannot be your own best friend when things go awry on the course, you will not only have difficulty overcoming the varied obstacles on the golf course, but you may also become a victim of your own self-hatred. Think about the negative self-talk you've had with yourself. It's easy to say horrible things to ourselves from time to time. So, ask yourself this: *Is this something I would say to a good friend who just hit the same bad shot that I did?* Of course not! If that is true, then why in the world would you ever say such a negative thing to yourself?

SELF-COMPASSION

Self-compassion is what develops once our self-talk is consistently positive in nature. Self-compassion is simply treating yourself with the kindness and dignity you give those you love and care about. Self-compassion is not the same as self-esteem. Self-esteem can cover up personal flaws by making broad positive statements such as "I am a nice person" or "I am a great putter." You may generally be a nice person or even a great putter—but when you yell at someone for no good reason or experience an atrocious day on the greens, then what? Chasing self-esteem can pose issues when relying on outcomes that are intended to match up with the self-concept. Since outcomes are often unpredictable, working on self-esteem based on them is not effective.

According to a study on self-esteem by Kristin D. Neff, "Self-esteem is largely the outcome of doing well, not the cause of doing well. For instance, self-esteem appears to be the result rather than the cause of improved academic performance." She points out that although there have been a number of large-scale programs to promote self-esteem in schools, many of these self-esteem programs for school kids tend to emphasize indiscriminate praise. Elementary schools in particular assume that their mission is to raise the self-esteem of their pupils in order to prepare children for success and happiness later in life. For this reason, they discourage teachers from making critical remarks to young children because of the damage it might do to their self-esteem.

The desire to raise children's self-esteem has led to some serious grade inflation. Forty-eight percent of high-school students received an A average in 2004, as compared to eighteen percent in 1968. So, is all this emphasis on raising self-esteem actually a good thing? Not necessarily.

Self-compassion, as opposed to self-esteem, means recognizing and accepting all of your blemishes, while appreciating the positives you possess. One huge advantage of practicing self-compassion over self-esteem is that it is available precisely when self-esteem fails us—when we go out and shoot a terrible score and feel embarrassment. Studies have shown that self-compassion lessens the "threat system" (defensiveness and self-doubt) and activates the "self-comforting" system. While self-compassion is linked with well-being because it makes people feel safe and protected, self-esteem makes people feel superior and confident.

Because of this, self-compassion is not just more honest, it is more genuine. Golf, particularly tournament golf, highlights our shortcomings. Therefore, self-compassion must go hand in hand with being your own BFF. You've been criticizing yourself for years, and it's been preventing you from being your best—a Tournament Golfer. You'll always be a work in progress, so give yourself a break by valuing the positives along with accepting the the negatives.

FORGIVENESS

Forgiveness might be the second cousin to self-compassion, but it is a bit different. The forgiveness I'm talking about is self-forgiveness—and it has to start before you actually commit the action that needs your forgiveness! What do I mean?

It goes like this: We are human beings and so, by definition, we will screw up. A lot. On top of that, we've chosen to play the game of golf, which was seemingly invented to highlight our weaknesses. Once we recognize that we are all destined to make mistakes, then it is easier to forgive ourselves *in advance*. Every mistake is a valuable lesson—and when framed as such, moves us ever closer to accomplishing our goal. We learn from mistakes; thus we improve.

Mistakes can inspire you to make progress and, if handled correctly, play a significant role in making you better in the long run. We are human. We are mistake-making machines. Get over it. Forgive yourself and drive on.

GOLF DOESN'T DEFINE YOU AS A PERSON

I have to be honest here. In my case, this is not 100 percent true. Golf is such a big part of who I am that it is disingenuous to say golf doesn't play some role in who I am. There have been a few times in my life when I realized I had let the game climb too high on my list of important stuff in my life. For a serious golfer, this situation is going to happen from time to time, so it's a good idea to keep a lookout for it when it happens.

In my experience, this feeling of golf defining yourself comes from really good golf—or really bad golf. When you win an event, you naturally feel good about yourself. When you bomb out in a tournament, you feel like a dog. My advice is to be aware of this tendency and avoid letting yourself get too high of an opinion of yourself with the wins—or too low with the poor performances. Make the effort to keep things in perspective and avoid letting results dominate your persona.

If need be, take a break and get away from the game when it starts to play too big of a role in who you are. Golf is bigger than all of us, but we get to choose how big it is in our life.

I made a 10 on a par-five final hole in a state championship one year. Nice way to finish. Lucky for me, I was not in contention that year. Was I embarrassed? You bet. All of my friends wanted an immediate recalling of every shot from one to ten. As a younger man, posting a score in the 80s was devastating. I let the bad result creep into defining who I was as a person. This time, I was much older, and had more mental scar tissue to help deflect the pain, so it was easier to laugh it off and put it in the rear-view mirror. This 10 was not going to define me. This is what the Tournament Golfer does so well.

Jack Nicklaus, the greatest golfer of all time, was asked in an interview what was the one thing he wanted to be remembered for. The questioner was expecting something like, "My eighteen major championships" or "My victory in the '86 Masters at age forty-eight." But Jack said, "I want to be remembered as a good father." If Jack Nicklaus chooses not to let golf be the sole definition of who he is, neither should we.

PERSPECTIVE

The above is also about perspective, but there's more. It's easy to let golf climb to the top of the list of what our lives are all about, forgetting it's just a game we play. Especially true for the young Tournament Golfers, lack of perspective typically leads to burnout and total disillusionment. In some cases, these disheartened kids quit playing altogether. I have witnessed this scenario more than once, and it was always with junior golfers. Perspective was difficult for them to acquire.

One such Tournament Golfer was a few years younger than I. His name was David. We were both "Range Rats," spending all our after-school time at a local driving range. The outside flood lights at this range would automatically turn off at closing time, 10:00 P.M. There were numerous times that a putt was hit across the green in a tight putting match at 9:59:59 and we would have to run in the dark after the still-rolling ball to access the result.

David turned into the best twelve-year-old golfer in the state of California. He played in hundreds of tournaments and won seventy percent of them. I remember a photo of him kneeling in front of a mountain of trophies. He was a world beater who, in many people's opinion, became the best junior golfer California ever produced. I convinced him to consider joining the golf team at the University of Houston soon after I graduated. He flew to Houston to tour the school and meet everyone. But he decided to attend another university.

David put a tremendous amount of pressure on himself, and much was expected of him. In the middle of his freshman year, he reached the burnout stage and quit golf for good. With golf being the total sum of his life at his young age, its departure from his daily routine left an enormous void in his life. He filled the void with a new bad group of friends and the drugs they introduced him to. I never heard from David again, but I heard that he had hit rock bottom and stayed there. A little perspective in David's life would have saved him from this fate—and everyone reading this book would know his name.

Perspective comes from experience and a recognition of the world around you. As you already know, my golf team won the NCAA championship in 1977. What you couldn't know is that on the 72nd hole of that tournament, I hit a beautiful shot twelve feet below the hole for a birdie opportunity. I knew we were either in the lead or very close to it. The next hour would tell what team was to be crowned National Champion. Every shot carried incredible weight. I was not a Tournament Golfer yet, and all I could think about was the result of winning or losing the National Championship, and that I must do my part!

I stepped over the putt trying to make the birdie that might lift my team to the title. I ran it by the hole a couple of feet and missed it coming back. I felt I had singlehandedly sunk my team's chances to win. In my head, I could hear all 35,000 students at the University of Houston groan in unison over my careless 3-putt bogey. I had let them down, too. I was a senior, so there was no "get 'em next year." There wasn't going to be a next year. My college career had just ended with the choke stroke of all time. To this day, I have never been more furious with myself.

I headed over to the locker room at a breakneck pace and slammed open the door leading into it and proceeded up the stairs to my locker. As I glanced up, there was a teenage boy struggling with his two crutches to make his way down the stairs toward me. They weren't the sort of crutches one uses when one has a sprained ankle or knee. These crutches were custom fit, and it was obvious this boy had permanent mobility issues. He was severely handicapped. In this moment of clarity—of perspective—I felt the anger and despair drain out of me like someone had just poked a water balloon with a pin. Instinctively, I knew I had no right or license to feel sorry for myself. I recognized instantly what a difficult life this young man had had up to this point and how much tougher it could well be for the rest of his life.

I received instantaneous perspective at the moment I needed it the most. I was grateful then for this gift of perspective and I remain grateful still.

Golf is just a game. Don't let it own you.

RESILIENCE

The definition of *resilient* is the ability to recover quickly from difficulties. This can mean recovery from a poor swing, or it can mean overcoming a longer-term challenge. It is a mental toughness that allows the Tournament Golfer to bounce back from adversity. Being your own best friend is at the core of resilience. You also need to have a support system of people who care about you.

But true resilience all starts from within. Resiliency doesn't happen after the fact; it is a decision you make in advance. Resiliency is a mental perspective you put in place prior to making the bad swing or the bad decision. You know it's coming and you have decided in advance to respond to it in a resilient way.

One year in the Texas State Amateur, I set out with a primary goal to avoid beating myself up over poor shots or scores. I have never been accused of being a perfectionist, but most of my golfing life I have demanded much from myself. I thought this was how the great players acted. A secondary goal of this tourney was to avoid making any big numbers. This goal came about because I found myself in this unexplainable cycle of making doubles and triples in an otherwise solid round of golf. These big numbers seem to come out of nowhere, and they would blow me out of contention. I was determined to play it safe and not blow my rounds up with these damaging scores.

The very 1st hole of the State Am this year was a par five, and I made a triple-bogey 8. First hole! Failing at my secondary goal was immediately out of the way, so I could focus on achieving my primary goal. I have to say, I did not get upset with myself nor did I succumb to becoming a victim. I kept my cool and, though disappointed, I was determined to rebound and see this thing through.

I did not win the Texas State Am that year, but I did finish ninth and I was my own best friend all week. I showed resilience. Mahatma Gandhi said, "We may stumble and fall but we shall rise again; it should be enough if we did not run away from the battle."

Life Hack

There is immense power in being your own best friend. Self-talk is a part of that, but there is much more to it than just words. The people closest to you—your spouse, parents, or kids—will never make you completely whole. Your occupation will never make you whole, either. Possessions will certainly never make you whole. Your relationship with yourself will be the longest relationship in the history of your life. To be whole, you must learn to respect and appreciate yourself. To be whole, you must understand that you are worthy. To be whole, you must stop punishing yourself. Finally, to be whole, you must focus on the positives about yourself and not obsess about the negatives.

Being your own best friend and showing kindness to yourself has obvious benefits. But it also has verified health benefits. "Harsh self-criticism activates the sympathetic nervous system—fight or flight—and elevates stress hormones such as cortisol in our bloodstream," says Emma Seppälä, PhD, author of *The Happiness Track*. "[T]oo much cortisol can lead to problems ranging from weight gain to cardiovascular trouble. Treat yourself the way you'd treat a friend who's going through a hard time—with support and understanding, instead of criticism."

Other studies have found that using self-compassion techniques can reverse the negative trend of criticism and cortisol. "When you practice self-compassion, you reduce the stress hormone cortisol, which takes away the state of stress," says Deborah Serani, PhD, award-winning author of *Living with Depression* and a psychology professor at Adelphi

University. "The more you stay with positive thoughts, the more dopamine surges, which floods your body with feel-good hormones."

Be your own best friend.

13
WHERE ARE YOU TAKING YOUR GOLF?

People do not decide to become extraordinary.
They decide to accomplish extraordinary things.

—Sir Edmund Hillary

THE SUPER-POWER OF SMALL WINS

In his book, *Atomic Habits*, James Clear writes about behaviors reflecting one's identity. Clear says to decide the type of person you want to be, and then prove it to yourself with small wins. Audacious goals can be accomplished with continuous small improvements in the direction of that goal.

For example: If a player tends to get angry at a poor shot or bad break and realizes this behavior is counterproductive, they can begin to cure it with "small wins." Let's say a player dumps a second shot in the lake in front of the green. They feel their heartbeat increase, slam the club on the ground, shout an expletive, and throw the club in anger. When a player has made the decision to reel in their anger as an important goal to achieve, the first small win might be to pledge to never throw a club again. They may get upset at the next opportunity, yet hang on to that club. When time goes by, and they have been successful in not winging the club when upset, the next win might be to vow not to shout out an obscenity, and so on. By stringing together small wins, the goal of staying calm when bad stuff happens can be achieved.

A Stanford University study found that large, abstract goals create "greater psychological distress, such as anxiety and depression." At the same time, the study found that individuals who made smaller, concrete goals showed higher happiness levels. The study found that those who set intermediate goals and then switched to the overall goal were more productive than those who focused only on the intermediate goals or only on overall goals.

The super-power of small wins is that they allow you to concentrate on the *how* of accomplishing a goal rather than *what* the next actionable step in the process might be. Since the intermediate goal is more realistic and manageable, you attain feedback more rapidly. Additionally, as small wins are checked off, motivation is enhanced, and a solid foundation of confidence is slowly developed.

My favorite example of behavior reflecting identity is the example in *Atomic Habits* of two people with the goal of quitting smoking. When each is offered a cigarette, one says, "No thanks, I'm trying to quit," while the other one says, "No thanks, I'm not a smoker." The second person has made the decision to be a nonsmoker and their behavior is now reflecting their new identity.

To become a Tournament Golfer, you must first start *acting* like one. Create small wins by practicing those behaviors that make you a Tournament Golfer: being present, being your own best friend, surrendering to the outcome, taking responsibility, and so on.

In other words, assume that identity. Pile up small wins until you are a full-fledged Tournament Golfer.

Clear also discusses systems vs. goals. He writes, "Eventually, I began to realize that my results had very little to do with the goals I set and nearly everything to do with the systems I followed." Clear is a process guy, too. "Goals are about the results you want to achieve. Systems are about the processes that lead to those results."

The goal in any sport is to finish with the best score, but it would be ridiculous to spend the entire game staring at the scoreboard. "Goals are for setting direction," Clear concludes, "but systems are best for making progress." What a fitting description of the Tournament Golfer.

Life Hack

Decide what goal you wish to achieve. Be clear about it. Do you really want this goal? If it has been on your radar for some time and you don't seem to be any closer, it's time to do something different. Tweak your strategy. Tweaking your approach may mean you just need to back up a step to a more intermediate system, which will lead to the next system in line toward your goal. You may have inadvertently leap-frogged over an important step en route to the goal. It is never a straight line. One thing is for sure: There is some reason you haven't achieved your selected goal. Identify it.

A common reason for individuals who fail to reach their goal is that they are too stuck on past failures. It's important to understand and acknowledge those missteps. Take what you learned from them and apply them to your process. Told your girlfriend, "Yes, you're right, those jeans do make your butt look bigger"? Mistake! Lost your cue cards right before a big speech? Mistake! So, your new process when asked about how she looks in her jeans might be to answer in the positive: "I love those jeans." Big speech or presentation coming up? Tweak your process so that your cue cards are right under your wallet or car keys, making them impossible to forget.

The point is not to think of any past failures as *who you are*. They were mistakes; you *learned* from them, and now you're *done* with them. Rather than say, "I'm awkward in social settings," you should be saying, "I was awkward at the dinner party, and I won't do that again. Instead, this is what I'll say next time. . . ." Box up your past disappointments. Make them ancient history.

14

POST-ROUND DEBRIEF

I never learned anything from a match I've won.

—Bobby Jones

Debriefing after a competitive round is vital element of growth and improvement. While it is probably true that we learn more from our mistakes, we can also learn from what we did right. Often, there is plenty of positive activity that occurred—even during a poor round—and it is important to understand why. This process requires us to relive every shot of the round and evaluate it. If it was a poor performance, this debrief can be full of regret. If it was a great performance, there is vital analysis to be performed, as well.

Most Golfers-Who-Play-Tournaments who conduct a debrief tend to be negative, spending their time with a degree of self-loathing and regret. It's difficult to be positive when performing a proper debrief—but beating yourself up is certainly counterproductive. The Tournament Golfer is clinical, more objective. They know that a post-tournament debrief is an opportunity to avoid repeating the same mistakes again. And that is their primary focus in their analysis.

To be successful in post-round debriefs, the player must have the ability to mentally recall all aspects of their performance. They must be realistic and honest about the round just played.

They must be self-reflective, positive, and dispassionate. There are two types of analysis in a post-round debrief.

Physical Analysis

This type is primarily identifying what aspect of your contact with the ball was good or poor. For example, you may have had too many 3-putt greens. Was it because your iron play consistently put your ball too far from the hole, increasing the likelihood of a 3-putt? Was your stroke just off that day and you were mis-hitting putts? Perhaps you struggled with reading of the greens. What was it exactly that was the root of the 3-putts? Once you establish what it was that caused the poor performance, focus on shoring up that particular physical deficiency in your next practice session.

Mental Analysis

This analysis is often centered around decisions made that resulted in a poor outcome. This might be as simple as hitting too much or not enough club into a green. It could be playing too aggressively by going at "sucker pins" where the penalty is too great if the shot misses the mark by a small amount. It could simply be the recognition of getting out of the present, or letting a bad pairing upset you.

When the mental analysis of the post-round debrief is successful, you will confirm suspicions you had before the debrief, and some new discoveries may show up during. In either event, a decision must be made to correct those mental errors. For example, if you find that your approach shots were mostly short of the hole, make the decision to hit the extra club tomorrow when stuck between clubs. If you are missing fairways more than usual, perhaps lay up on the shorter holes.

I have found it useful to have a friend or teacher take part in my debriefs. It needs to be someone who has some tournament golf experience, and who cares about you and your golf. It's good to get someone else's take on what happened in your round because they can view it from the outside, and they might have had a similar experience that they can share with you on how they fixed it.

As I mentioned earlier, reviewing great shots and decisions in the post-round debrief is important, too. Reliving them burns them into your subconscious memory, which builds confidence and makes them available to draw upon when a similar shot or decision is required in a future round.

For you to have a successful post-round debrief, it's essential that you have a confidant who cares about you, knows you, and understands your golf game. For me, this person was the previously mentioned gym coach, Lee Myers. He was a great player and competitor in his own right. Coach was a scratch golfer, Golden Gloves boxer, and even a pitcher in the Brooklyn Dodgers organization for a time. He was the only person I looked to whenever my tournament golf went sideways. He was the ideal confidant because he never let me pull him into my victimhood. He would be empathetic and at the same time offer tough love. Whether he was there to watch me play or not, we would go over every shot hit—and he'd ask me what I was thinking, and what was my intention for every shot. He kept me honest and held me responsible. This is the sort of person you should look for in order to have a successful post-round debrief.

Life Hack

At my firm, we work hard at institutionalizing the way we do things. This process makes us better at everything we do by lessening the chance for error. Just like an airline pilot and co-pilot who make systems checks before a flight and afterwards, we spend time before and after client presentations making sure we offered up our best. As a young financial advisor, I made all the boneheaded mistakes possible. But I learned from them by having a "business post-round debrief," attending to those aspects of my presentation that needed improvement.

My typical presentation would entail an extensive explanation of financial markets and how I had a plan for the prospective client's money to benefit from my thoughtful advice. It wasn't until I started bringing other advisors into the meetings with me that I discovered that my presentations were generic, just like any other financial advisor—a "features and benefits" presentation. I knew I needed to make a change. I didn't know it yet, but what I needed was to turn my mirror into a window and focus on what the prospective client really needed in their financial life—not on all the great things I could do for them.

Through my business post-round debriefs, I slowly began to recognize that I had to ask more questions and do less talking. I needed to find out what it was in the prospective client's financial life, and in their daily life, that was stressing them out enough that they would seek a financial advisor in the first place. I finally learned that it wasn't about *me*, it was about *them*.

Post-round debriefs are an essential tool—on the golf course and off.

15

FIND A MENTOR

A lot of people have gone further than they thought they could because someone else thought they could.

—Zig Ziglar

YOU NEED A TEAM

Don't go it alone. Golf is a lonely game, so you need a team. Your team can be just you and your coach, like it was for Coach Myers and me. You need trusted input—someone to help bear the load that golf places upon all Tournament Golfers. Just as it is vital to have a post-round debrief with a trusted person, it is important to have a teacher, a mentor to guide you along. It can be that same trusted person who analyzes your golf game with you, or it can be a totally different person.

Mentors are there to offer encouragement in those down times when golf is beating you up. This encouragement has great value in and of itself; but a mentor offers much more. A mentor offers up their own experience for you to draw upon, to plug into. They have been down this path before, and they know where the potholes are.

A mentor reminds you to keep your eye on the big picture, on the goal. Goals are easy to forget when we get negative. A mentor will draw attention to the progress made up to this point, reminding the Tournament Golfer that there are many speedbumps along the way, and a down period is just one of them. A mentor also keeps you accountable by not granting excuses. They should listen to your excuses, of course, but not buy into them or dwell on them.

I believed in myself because Coach Myers believed in me. When he introduced me to golf that fateful day at the summer sports camp, he may have seen something in me. Or maybe he just decided to call the bluff of this smart-ass kid who was not going to give the game a shot by walking home. It doesn't really matter. Like all great mentors, his first step was taking an interest in me. In my particular case, our connection grew into something much deeper: a father-and-son relationship.

WORKING WITH AN INSTRUCTOR

We all need help with our golf game. Working with a good golf instructor is essential to improvement. The most important aspect of your relationship with your golf coach is compatibility. Having a similar belief system about golf and how it should be played is more important than the lessons you might get. Your instructor must also be able to relate to your individual needs, so communication is crucial, too.

Carol Mann—World Golf Hall of Fame inductee and Women's Open Champion—was my instructor for many years, and she taught me so much. When I would refer a friend of mine to get a lesson from Carol, I cautioned them to have the answer to her opening question, "What do you want to accomplish with your golf?" If you did not have a good answer to this question, there might not be a lesson at all that day.

Carol told me about a young man she met on a flight to Houston who immediately recognized her. He politely walked up to her row, introduced himself, and asked if she would consider giving him a lesson when they got back to Houston. "What do you want to accomplish with your golf?" she asked. He said that he wasn't really sure. Carol asked him to go back to his seat, and when he figured that out, she would be glad to visit with him about giving him a lesson. Carol absolutely wanted her students to be goal-oriented!

Some golf instructors are "method" teachers so that the answer to a student's swing challenges is always the same: "Adopt my swing method and all will be fine." There are other golf instructors who diagnose a student's flaws and go about offering a solution without requiring the student to adopt their swing dogma. I have always appreciated the hybrid golf instructor—someone who has a belief system regarding how a club should be swung but who is flexible enough to adapt to the idiosyncrasies of the student's swing. The reality is, some students cannot adapt to a teacher's swing theory, but they still need their help. Many tour players break up with their swing coaches because they finally discover that they can't really switch to the instructor's swing philosophy.

A few years before her death, I went to Carol and told her that I had about five basic swings, and that I'd had success with all five of them at one time or another. I asked her to spend an entire day with me, pick the swing that she thought was best for me, and I would drop the other swings to concentrate on perfecting the swing she chose. Carol said she would not do it. She went on to tell me that even the greatest players of all time had multiple swings. She told me that a Tournament Player had to be adaptive above all else. When in a tournament and a particular swing is not getting the job done, a player must try another method to solve the poor shots—or risk blowing themselves out of the tournament.

Life Hack

In everything you do, it benefits you to seek the guidance of one who has walked this path before. Seek a mentor in all you do. The benefits are:

- You save time by avoiding mistakes that need not be made, thus accelerating your improvement
- You have increased confidence
- You achieve greater awareness of other methodologies
- You have a confidential sounding-board for ideas and challenges
- A mentor maintains accountability
- A mentor listens and cares

16
FINAL THOUGHTS

Thinking is easy, acting is difficult, and to put one's thoughts into action is the most difficult thing in the world.
—Johann Wolfgang von Goethe

DANCE WITH THE ONE THAT BRUNG YA (PLAN B)

Carol Mann was a Tournament Golfer as well as a gifted instructor. She was unique in that after we worked on my swing mechanics, she would give me an alternative swing key—for the possibility that, in the middle of a tournament round, all the work we had just done failed to succeed. She was all about winning tournaments! A "method" instructor doesn't offer a Plan B. Their answer is always just to work harder perfecting their method, and all will go well.

No method works all the time, and Carol understood this truth. There are times when you can go through every swing method you have in your arsenal and none of them will work. An example of this was the second collegiate tournament I ever played in. It was hosted by Baylor University in Waco, Texas. I had been playing pretty well and was looking forward to the event. But in the practice round, out of nowhere, I was hitting a twenty-yard hook with every swing. Even my wedge shots were bending hard left. I tried everything I could, but the dreaded shrimp would not relent. When it was time to start the tournament, I finally had to give up on trying to banish my hook and just play for it.

This situation meant I had to aim my driver in the right trees, and it would come snapping back into the fairway. At times this hook was so extreme that it would cross the fairway from right to left and run into the left rough. All of my approach shots hit the green and ran left, so I had to under-club by a full club to allow for the run out. It was embarrassing. But I had no choice. Anyway, I found myself in a playoff to win the tournament. I hit a thirty-yard hook off the tee that ended up in the fairway, and made a twenty-five-foot birdie putt from just left of the pin to win. Sometimes you just have to dance with the one that brung ya!

Indeed, I saw an interview with Johnny Miller about his historic 63 in the fourth round of the 1973 U.S. Open at Oakmont. He had put a 76 up on the board in the third round to place himself well off the lead, six strokes back. He said that by the 3rd hole of the final round, he had to totally abandon the swing keys he had used in the first three rounds. He adapted and went with another one of his swings. The result? He hit all eighteen greens in regulation for his historic 8 under 63 to win by a shot.

So, Carol was right. Go with the swing that is working. There are three interesting sidenotes about Mr. Miller's historic round:

1. He lipped out his birdie putt for a 62 on 18 that day.
2. Johnny cashed the U.S. Open winner's check of $35,000. At this year's Players Championship at Sawgrass, the winner received $3.6 million—a 100-fold increase from '73.
3. Miller had won only two tour events prior to the 1973 U.S. Open. He went on to win twenty-three more, including another major.

WRITE DOWN AND SAVE YOUR SWING KEYS

I'm not a big stat keeper, but I keep notes on the swing keys I am working on. Importantly, I date them or title them by the event I was playing in when using them. While swing keys will evolve with our knowledge of our particular golf swing, it's also easy to get away from those keys that were working well enough to have brought a first-place trophy home. By keeping notes on swing keys by date or event, I can more easily get back on track by referring to them. I have noticed that some swing keys that worked last month no longer work as well this month. It's as if their warranty ran out. That's okay, because if the swing key was significant in the past, it will likely be of use in the future. I have also noticed that some past swing keys keep showing up on my current list. That's also okay. It means they are relevant. Keep them close.

CADDIES

Caddies are great. But, like swing coaches or post-round debrief confidants, they should not offer excuses for your bad play or your unfortunate on-course decisions. This is a tall order for a caddie because the player they typically loop for is looking for sympathy, for someone to acknowledge their victimhood. Caddies who approve of and buy into the players' excuses tend to get paid more. Get a caddie who knows you and refuses to put up with any victimhood you might offer in your weakest moments. If your caddie confirms your victimhood, they hollow out your ability to take responsibility or to embrace the suck.

MATCH PLAY

We all know that match play is radically different from medal play. The player who brings a medal-play mindset to their matches will experience considerably improved match-play results. As I have stressed up to this point, the key to being in the present is process. Avoid thinking in terms of results. In match play, we are now going head to head with another player and thus the opportunities to be pulled out of the present increase exponentially.

Our opponent hits their approach shot five feet from the hole or bombs their drive right down the middle, and now it's our turn. Not only do we have the usual external pressure of hitting our shot over a lake or sand trap, but we also now have our opponent's ball up tight to the pin or crushed down the middle. The Golfer-Who-Plays-Tournaments feels they must now stick their ball close to the hole or crush their drive down the middle. This is not process-oriented golf; this is fear mixed with results-oriented golf.

In match play, work your process exactly like you do in a non-match play environment. You have no control over what your opponent is doing, so don't let their actions pull you out of the present.

It is worth mentioning that it isn't really the great shot your match-play opponent hits up close to the hole that messes with your mind. When this happens, there is a certain amount of surrendering to the outcome and you may lose the hole, so just do your best and see what happens. Far more damaging to your ability to stay in the present is when your opponent hits a really poor shot, and now you anticipate the win. If your opponent sails their shot over the green or buries their ball on the greenside bunker, we are pulled away from our process into thinking about a result: *All I have to do is slap it up on the green somewhere for the easy win.* And then you hit it thirty feet and 3-putt—and they make the fifteen-foot putt for par to win the hole. Assuming a sure-win result due to our opponent's poor shot is just as bad, or worse, than the good shot they hit pulling us out of the present.

Work your process no matter what your opponent does. Stay present.

Never accept a "good-good" suggestion from your match-play opponent. A good-good offer is when you both have short putts and you are asked to consider your opponent's putt holed and, in return, they will concede your remaining putt. The reason they are offering is not to be charitable to you. They are so worried about getting a bad result with their putt that they are willing to give you a good result. Don't fall for it. Except when both putts are a foot or less, refuse the good-good when offered. You have an excellent chance to prevail—as your opponent is not in the present. They are in results-oriented mode, and therefore they're vulnerable. Just say, "No, thanks."

PICKING YOUR SCORE ON THE 1ST TEE

Most golf commentators are pretty good at what they do—but they will ask questions that make it obvious they were never Tournament Golfers. I'm not talking about Johnny Miller or Nick Faldo; they were two of the best Tournament Golfers ever. No, I'm talking about those announcers who may have cut their teeth announcing football or baseball, and their producers assume they can cover golf tournaments just as well.

For example, how many times has a golf commentator asked a tour player on the eve of the final round, "So, what do you need to shoot tomorrow to win this thing?" The players often play along and give their questioner a number. But to my mind, these Tournament Golfers will not be thinking about score too much while on the course. They will be working their process, not fixating on a score that shifts them into results-oriented thinking.

I have been guilty of picking a score, particularly in various qualifiers over the years. For instance, when I was in my forties, I entered the local U.S. Mid-Am qualifier. It was really hard for me not to think of a pre-determined score because there were just four spots to be awarded, and the starting field was ninety-two players. I felt I needed to break par—or maybe I could get away with shooting even to get a spot. This was on my mind all day. Coming into the last few holes I was one over par. I needed some birdies. I started shooting at pins and played the last three holes over par because of my overly aggressive play. I knew I needed to squeeze a birdie or two out of my round coming in, but instead I went the other way and shot 74.

When I got in, I saw that the scores were not as low as I expected. In fact, 73 got in without a playoff. How foolish I had been. I had allowed a pre-determined score to fill my head all day and fell into a results-oriented mindset. So I played more aggressively than I should have, making a careless bogey on the finishing holes. I had thrown my process out the window along with a spot in a national championship.

In 1978, I was twenty-two years old and the youngest player on the PGA Tour. In a previous chapter, you'll recall I secured my tour card the prior November, getting my ball up and down from the back bunker on 18 at Pinehurst Number Four to save bogey. Anyway, here I was at The New Orleans Open in Gretna, Louisiana. In 1978, the Tour was not an "all-exempt" tour—as it became in 1983 and is today. Unless a "non-exempt" player made the 36-hole cut in the prior week's tour stop, we had to qualify on the Monday of the event. This applied to all players who were not within the top 125 on the tour's money list—even if you earned your tour card through the grueling Tour School qualifying school.

I was paired with Jim Colbert, a tour standout who was at the tail end of a solid career. Even though he was a tour player, he had lost his exempt status by dropping out of the top 125 on the money list. I was trying to find a way to get on that list. I was playing okay until I snap-hooked my tee shot out of bounds on hole 9 and made a triple bogey. In a one-day qualifier, a double bogey was usually a death blow to your chances of getting a spot.

A triple bogey? Forget about it. I stayed as positive as I could, working my process, but things looked pretty bleak. I was now four over par standing on the 13 tee.

Then, something interesting happened. I birdied 13. Colbert wasn't having a good day but kept encouraging me and telling me to keep my foot on the accelerator. I did. I birdied 14, 15, 16, and 17. Now I was one under par, which I reckoned would be good enough to snag one of the thirty open non-exempt spots that week. I had a twenty-footer on 18 to birdie out, but 2-putted for a 71. I glanced at the scoreboard, and it looked like I was going to play this week. There were still some players out on the course, but I drove off knowing I was going to be one of the lucky thirty qualifiers.

I needed some shaving cream and I was low on deodorant, so I went by a convenience store to pick up a new supply on my way back to my hotel room. I had a habit of leaving all of my shirts and slacks hanging on a long wooden dowel across the entire back seat of my car rather than bring all of them into my hotel room each night. As I walked out of the store, Paul Azinger was walking in. Seeing all of my shirts hanging in my backseat, Paul assumed I had not qualified and was on my way out of New Orleans to the next tour stop.

"Didn't get it done today, huh, Book?" he asked.

"No, no, I'm in," I said. "Shot 71."

"Man, Mike, when I left, I think 71 was in a playoff," Paul responded.

My heartbeat went into overdrive as I felt a massive shot of adrenaline flow through my every fiber. There were no cell phones in 1978, but I saw a pay phone at the other end of the parking lot. I sprinted over to it, but there was no phone book to look up the number of the club I had left thirty minutes before. My hands were shaking wildly as I put a dime in and dialed information,

411. I got the number of the club and started punching the numbers in. I misdialed three or four times, my fingers feeling like five jumbled rubber bands.

When I finally got the number right, the young assistant pro in the golf shop answered the phone.

"Lakewood Golf Shop, how may I help you?"

I asked him what score it took today to qualify.

He answered, "I think 71 was in a playoff. Let me doublecheck." And then he put me on hold.

What am I going to tell my financial backer? *"Well, instead of staying around after my round to make sure I qualified, I left to go buy shaving cream."* *What an idiot you are*, repeated the voice in the back of my head over and over. *What was I thinking?*

Still on hold for what seemed an eternity, I continued to beat myself up for being so careless, so naïve.

"Nope, 71 is in, 72 played off," said the voice at the other end of the line.

If I had been on hold much longer, I think I might have wet my pants. I was in after all.

Here was another example of the danger of picking a score in advance and anchoring yourself to it. This results-oriented thinking almost sunk me *after* the fact. Ironically, I had just done a great job of working my process on the course—making five birdies in a row to flip disaster into triumph.

I was more than fortunate to compete in the event that week, and I learned an important lesson. It ain't over 'til it's over!

TEAM GOLF

Team golf is the toughest format of all tournament golf because you suffer individually for a bad performance, *and* you suffer for hurting your team—the double whammy. If that's not enough, when you perform like a champion, other members of the team may not—and effectively nullify your nice score. I'm referring to the medal-play format that most colleges and universities play, not the match-play format of a Walker Cup or Ryder Cup.

Now, I admit, the pressure the Walker and Ryder Cups have on their participants is enormous. Players carry the weight of their respective countries on their shoulders. Likewise, the entire golfing world knows every shot they hit, good or bad, in real time. But in team golf, each team must use the best four-out-of-five scores of their players and add them together. If you lose a match in the Ryder Cup, it hurts your team's cause, for sure, but one player won't take the entire team down, as they are one of twelve players, and their score doesn't get added to their teammate's scores.

But in the college medal-play format, one team member represents twenty percent of the team; and if their performance is bad enough, the fourth-best score must be counted and added to the top three. If the fourth-best score is bad enough, the number-five man just sunk the rest of the team. Game over.

Let me tell you, it was a long ride back to the hotel from the tournament site for the guy on the team who blew up his scorecard that day. Sometimes that guy was me—and when it was, I wanted to crawl into a hole and die. The current format of the Division One NCAA Championship is a blend of the medal- and match-play worlds, and I really like it. All teams compete in medal play until the top eight teams are seated. Then they go at each other in match play, like in the Ryder Cup.

MUSIC ON THE GOLF COURSE

At the risk of sounding like a fossil, music on the course is a distraction away from what you are doing on the course. I don't know about you, but I love music; so when I hear a song, it takes me back in time to when I first heard it and where I was in my life at that time. If music engages you in some way, then you're not in the present. You're back in the past somewhere reliving some moment, if even for just an instant.

Sometimes music on the course just annoys you and provides an unwanted distraction. Like the guy I was paired with who played techno music—loudly. It doesn't take you out of the present like a song you remembered from your past. It just irritates you.

It's awkward to ask your playing partner to turn their music off, so what I suggest is this: If you are riding in a cart where the music is playing, drive to your cart partner's ball and walk over to yours. This way, you can gather yourself in the moment by getting out of earshot of the music and begin your pre-shot routine uninterrupted. Even when playing recreational golf, you want to be ready to hit a good shot. Going back in the past with one of your favorite tracks reduces the chances of a good shot.

DON'T WORRY ABOUT WHAT OTHERS THINK

A major part of the Tournament Golfer mindset is not caring about what others think. I have always found this to be difficult. In 1980, I played in the Kansas State Open. I was playing well and had a good pairing in the first round. On the 4th hole, I hit my ball in the fairway, but a sprinkler head had broken, and an area was marked off with a white circle, an indication that it was ground under repair—a free drop. I called over to my playing partners saying that my ball was inside the white line and that I was going to take a drop.

They waived back the okay sign and I picked up my ball, took the nearest clear point of relief, and dropped the ball. I stepped up to the ball and took my stance. I was about to make my swing when, out of the corner of my eye, I noticed that my left foot was partially inside the white line. I hadn't dropped it far enough outside the free drop area, which meant I had not actually taken relief. You must take relief once you have decided to take a drop. Once again, I motioned over to my playing partners that I had made a mistake and not taken adequate relief. I was going to have to drop again, this time, 100 percent out of the white circled drop area.

I hit my ball and went on to shoot a very competitive 69. When I got to the scorer's desk, one of my playing partners told the official I had made a bad drop. He contended that the only reason I made the second drop was because I didn't like the lie my ball landed in on the first drop, not because my foot was partially inside the ground under repair area as I had claimed. Our third player had no opinion as to the correctness of my drop. I denied his assertion and went on to explain why I felt compelled to re-drop my ball because it was the right thing to do. It had absolutely nothing to do with the lie my ball was in after the original drop.

Incredibly, the Kansas Golf Committee met for forty-five minutes to decide my fate.

Finally, an official came out to tell me, "We know you cheated, but it's his word against yours, so there will be no penalty or disqualification. But we've got our eye on you!" I was crestfallen. It felt like someone had punched me in the gut. The worst thing in the world of tournament golf is to be accused of cheating. I couldn't sleep at all that night. When I arrived at the course the next morning, it seemed like everyone was looking at me differently. When I arrived at the first tee to begin my round, I discovered two Kansas Golf Association officials were going to follow my group, ostensibly to make sure that if I cheated, they would catch me in the act. Surely, I must be thought of as a cheater for the state officials to chaperone me for the round.

I 3-putted two of the first three holes, as I just couldn't recover from the shame of the cheater accusation. I had a truly miserable week, as the cheater cloud hung over me for the entire tournament. Remarkably, I tied Bob Tway for second place after the eventual winner chipped in for birdie on the last hole of the event to clip us by one. If I had been a true Tournament Golfer, I would not have been so thoroughly eaten up with the shame of what others thought of me. I would have risen above the situation and focused on taking care of business—working the process. I might have even won the Kansas Open. I just couldn't do it.

NOBODY REALLY CARES (VERY MUCH)

According to Wendy Rose Gould, "As humans, we are inherently hyper-focused on ourselves. We're worried that everyone's judging our bad-hair day, that lingering mustard stain, or the dust and cat hair that somehow made its way onto the computer screen right before a presentation. In reality, nobody notices the extra frizz in your hair, your coworkers are oblivious to your condiment mishap, and those dust particles are par for the course. Even if people did notice, they wouldn't really care because, well, they're likely too busy worrying about their own issues."

Gould is talking about the spotlight effect. The *spotlight effect* is "the tendency to feel and behave as if we are the focus of attention from an 'audience' that shares our preoccupations and insecurities about ourselves," explains Dr. Emma D. Levine, a cognitive therapist. "This imaginary audience is typically experienced as a potential threat insofar as we may be experienced negatively," she notes. "This is why, when we feel under the spotlight, we often experience uncomfortable emotional states, such as heightened self-consciousness or distortions in how we imagine others may view us."

Dr. Helen Odessky, a psychologist and author of *Stop Anxiety from Stopping You*, explains that this tendency is residual hardwiring from those primitive days when identifying friend or foe was essential to our survival. A lifesaver back then, perhaps, but in the modern world, it's a nuisance—with the potential for making things worse.

The cure is to find a way to step out of the spotlight. Consider:

- You're not a mind reader. According to Gould, "We all live inside our heads, and we also have a propensity toward irrational thinking." We become so accustomed to our internal thoughts that they start to feel unquestionably realistic. Many psychologists have written about the types of errors, or distortions, in the thinking of people who feel vulnerable to the impact of the spotlight effect. "One common example," Levine points out, "is 'mind reading,' or the tendency to believe that you know what others are thinking, thereby failing to consider other, more likely, possibilities."

- How often do you actually think of others? "We all have to devote a considerable amount of our attention to our own lives," says Odessky. "Even when you notice someone's mistake or mishap, think about how much time you devote to it before moving on to something more pertinent to your own life." Not much. It's the same for us all.

- Anxiety decreases in a situation when we expose ourselves to that situation more frequently. I'm not saying you should intentionally go out and bomb in a tournament just to train yourself not to be afraid of what others think. Nevertheless, I have found that when I played in multiple tournaments in a row, I naturally put less emphasis on the outcome of one event over another and therefore I was thinking less about what others might think of my performance in them. I adapted.

- People do care about us, but never as much we think they should. We don't care about others as much as they think we should, either. This is human nature. When we fall into the trap of dreading what others might think about us, we are dragged away from the process-oriented thinking of the job at hand and we are transported into results-oriented thinking. It didn't work for me in Kansas, and it won't work anywhere else.

For the Tournament Golfer, however, the lack of people caring as much as we think they ought to could be beneficial. Why? Because part of our weak tournament performances can be due to our concern about what others might think. So guess what? You're worrying about something that doesn't even exist. When you play well in an event, focus on the fact that your good finish is reward enough.

I never felt I didn't receive enough praise when I won a tournament. I knew my name was going on the trophy and that was enough for me. If you agree, then you really shouldn't worry about what others think about your golf. If you play poorly and finish well down the list, no one cares as much as you think. If you win, you get a trophy.

GO DOWN SWINGING

I love this old adage that refers to a batter in baseball. The idea is that you don't want the third strike called on you with the bat on your shoulder. At least if you swing at the ball, you might catch a piece of it and maybe even get a hit. As a baseball player, it is a bad feeling to watch the ball hit the strike zone for a strikeout if you just stood back and watched. You are disappointed, your teammates are disappointed, and the fans are disappointed.

I like this saying for golf, but for a very different reason. When in a tournament and things are going terribly, it's easy for the Golfer-Who-Plays-Tournaments to "phone it in"—to get upset and just quit caring. They might even be miserable to play with for the other players in the group. The Tournament Golfer understands a great truth that the Golfer-Who-Plays-Tournaments does not: You must continue to seek your best golf through the adversity of a bad round in order to maintain and safeguard your self-respect.

Like the batter who loathes the fact that they didn't at least swing at that third strike, when things are going badly, the golfer who doesn't retain their discipline—by executing their pre-shot routine, staying in the present, being their own best friend, and so on—can lose respect for their actions and themselves. It is one thing to look back on a poor performance with regret, but it is something entirely different to look back on a round knowing that you gave up.

I know some golfers reading this will say, "Sometimes when I give up on a round, I start making better shots and drain more putts." There is some truth to this. What has happened? Their don't-give-a-shit-meter has gone off: They have surrendered to the coming bad outcome and given up on the result. There is a lesson here, too. Just like knocking in putt after putt on the practice green while talking to someone and just rolling the ball in the direction of the hole, a bad performance can teach us to forget about results and work our process instead.

Finish out every tournament round by maintaining your discipline, doing the best you can. If you let yourself give up when a round goes south, you whittle away at your self-respect. Confidence is built brick by brick and it is lost in the same way. When you diminish your self-respect, your confidence can suffer and cause additional issues—like slumps.

Finish every round out knowing you are a Tournament Golfer. Tournament Golfers go down swinging.

AFTERWORD

There is nothing for me to say about golf that hasn't already been said. All I really wanted to do was to make the distinction between the two types of golfers I have observed playing in tournaments for the last fifty-five years: *the Golfer-Who-Plays-Tournaments* and *the Tournament Golfer*. I wrote this book because I didn't think enough people were aware that these two golfers existed and understood the differences between them. I saw that even skilled golfers I knew were not thinking in terms of these two types of players and which they might be.

I also wanted to pay special tribute to my first golf coach, Lee Myers. I mentioned him several times because I owe so much to him. He changed the trajectory of my life by introducing me to the game. He wasn't just my golf coach; he was my mentor who was always there for me. He was so invested in my success in golf that when I won my first golf tournament, he cried like a baby. Here was a man's man—an accomplished Golden Gloves boxer, a former pitcher for the Brooklyn Dodgers, and a scratch golfer who cried tears of happiness at my success. I owe you, Coach!

While my father left our home when I was two, I had a very engaged mom, caring older siblings, and good friends growing up. But I lacked direction and never gave a thought about where I was going and didn't have any clue of how the world worked. As a young boy, my life was always just one bad decision away from going off the rails, and I could have easily become just another kid from a broken home who would slip through the cracks.

I often wonder what would have become of me had Coach Myers not led me to the game of golf. I'd probably still be in California, never making my way to Texas to join the golf team at the University of Houston, never winning a national championship. I never would have met my loving wife of forty-four years, Pat Booker, and by extension, my amazingly accomplished daughter Caitlin. Nor would I have ever been inducted into the Texas Golf Hall of Fame. If not for Coach Myers, my life would have been very different. Instead, my life has been filled with great joy and gratitude. I would not trade a minute of what it *has* been for what it *might* have been devoid of golf.

Most importantly, without tournament golf, I'd have never known the deep self-knowledge it provides and demands. There is nothing in my personal experience that has better prepared me for the curveballs of life than golf. This game has shown me just exactly who I am by exposing both my flaws and weaknesses, as well as uncovering my strengths and fortitude. Golf has insisted I play the ball as it lies—both on and off the golf course. And I am forever grateful.

I am a Tournament Golfer.

MIKE BOOKER
GOLF CAREER

- Inducted into the Texas Golf Hall of Fame 2019
- Winner of a record thirteen Texas Golf Association events, including Senior, Mid Am and Mid Am Match Play
- A record four-time Texas Golf Association Player of the Year (2012, 2014, 2015, and 2022, Senior)
- Two-time U.S. National Club Champion (2007 and 2008, Senior)
- Southern Texas PGA Amateur of the Year (2014)
- Two-time South Texas Player of the Year (STAGA)
- Texas Golf Association South Texas Player of the Year, all ages (2011)
- First/only golfer named Athlete of the Year, *Houston Sports News* (2002)
- A record eight-time Houston City Amateur and Senior Amateur Champion in three different decades (four amateur, four senior championships, 1985 to 2018)
- *GOLFWEEK* "Local Legends" selection-only, six golfers selected nationally (2014)
- Winner of Charlie Coe, Champions Cup (two times each), and Carlton Woods Invitational (a record four times)
- Playing Member, U. of Houston NCAA National Championship team (1977)
- Selected Associated Press NCAA All-American Team, U. of Houston (1977)
- Selected All Southwest Conference Team, U. of Houston (1977)

MIKE BOOKER
PROFESSIONAL CAREER

- Founded Financial Synergies Wealth Advisors, Inc. 1985
- Financial Services Industry designations:
  *Certified Financial Planner (**CFP**) 1986*
  *Chartered Financial Consultant (**ChFC**) 1988*
  *Certified Fund Specialist (**CFS**) 1992*
  *Board Certified in Asset Allocation (**BCAA**) 1995*
- Currently managing over $1,000,000,000 in client money
- Selected for *Worth Magazine*'s "Americas Top 200 Advisors" six times
- Selected for *The Financial Times*' "Top Registered Investment Advisers in America" multiple years
- Selected for the *Houston Business Journal*'s list of "Largest Houston-area Money Management Firms" multiple years
- Selected for *Forbes Magazine*'s "Elite Professional Directory," Forbes Top Managers of the U.S., multiple years
- Selected for *Wealth Manager*'s "Top Wealth Managers" multiple years
- Contributing author for *The Wealth Factor* and *Stop and Think*

Printed book and eBook available at:

For more information about
The Tournament Golfer's Playbook, visit:

tgplaybook.com

info@tgplaybook.com

For more information about Mike Booker
and playing like a Tournament Golfer, visit:

http://youtube.com/watch?v=vOwPYosr6Gg

https://twitter.com/texasgolfassoc/status/1416549639881437185?s=10

https://twitter.com/texasgolfassoc/
status/1416858564220620807?s=10

https://www.txga.org/2019/10/07/tga-stalwart-mike-booker-to-enter-
texas-golf-hall-of-fame/

https://www.dropbox.com/s/2rdwn7p1r50xph9/First%20Tee%20
2022_021022.mp4?dl=0

BIBLIOGRAPHY

Clear, James. *Atomic Habits: An Easy & Proven Way to Build Good Habits & Break Bad Ones.* New York: Avery Publishing Group, 2018.

Conners, Roger, Tom Smith, and Craig Hickman. *The Oz Principle: Getting Results Through Organizational and Individual Accountability.* New York: Penguin Group, 1994, 2004.

Csikszentmihalyi, Mihaly. *Evolving Self: A Psychology for the Third Millennium.* New York: Harper Perennial, 1994.

Maltz, Maxwell. *Psycho-Cybernetics: A New Way to Get More Living Out of Life.* New York: Simon & Schuster, 1960. This book has been updated and expanded many times since the original date of publication, but this is the one I read as a kid.

Mecca, Andrew, Neil Smelser, and John Vasconcellos, eds. *The Social Importance of Self-Esteem.* Oakland, Calif.: University of California Press, 1989.

Nagaraj, Vaishnavi. "10 Ways to Activate Your Subconscious Mind to Get What You Want." Firstcry.com. April 22, 2019. https://parenting.firstcry.com/articles/magazine-10-ways-to-activate-your-subconscious-mind-to-get-what-you-want/.

Neff, Kristin D. "Self-Compassion, Self-Esteem, and Well-Being." *Social and Personality Psychology Compass*, 5(1), (2011): 1–12.

Neff, Kristin D. and Vonk, Roos. "Self-Compassion Versus Global Self-Esteem: Two Different Ways of Relating to Oneself." *Journal of Personality* 77:1, February 2009.

Odessky, Helen. *Stop Anxiety from Stopping You: The Breakthrough Program for Conquering Panic and Social Anxiety*. Coral Gables, Fla.: Mango Publishing Group, 2017.

Seppälä, Emma. *The Happiness Track: How to Apply the Science of Happiness to Accelerate Your Success*. San Francisco: HarperOne, 2016.

Serani, Deborah. *Living with Depression: Why Biology and Biography Matter Along the Path to Hope and Healing*. Lanham, Md.: Rowman & Littlefield, 2011.

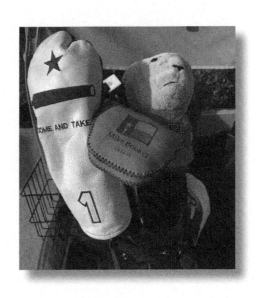